# THE BEST OF
# Birds&Blooms

# Contents

# From the editor

**It was another wonderful year** of colorful birds, butterflies and blooms! With all the gorgeous photos, helpful tips and expert advice to choose from, it was tough narrowing down our favorites from a year's worth of *Birds & Blooms* magazine. But we're thrilled to present this brand-new edition of *The Best of Birds & Blooms*. It's jam-packed with birding hints and tricks, easy do-it-yourself projects, gardening how-to's, stunning reader-submitted photos and more.

Discover how to make your backyard a hummingbird paradise with "Hello, Hummingbirds!" (page 84). Treat yourself to the juiciest, most delicious tomatoes ever when you follow the hints in "Grow a Terrific Tomato Crop" (page 210). Turn your next vacation into a birding adventure when you check out the hot spots in "Florida Birding from the Byways" (page 178).

You'll find all of this and more when you flip through *The Best of Birds & Blooms*. Whether you're passionate about gardening, birding, nature or all of the above, it's a collection to cherish.

*Kristen*

**KIRSTEN SWEET**
Editor, *Birds & Blooms*

Terrific Tomato
Crop (page 210)

Quick-to-Grow
Veggies (page 206)

©2018 RDA Enthusiast Brands, LLC
1610 N. 2nd Street, Suite 102, Milwaukee, WI 53212-3906
International Standard Book Number: 978-1-61765-743-6
International Standard Serial Number: 1553-8400
Component Number: 118500043H
All rights reserved.

Birds & Blooms is a registered trademark of
RDA Enthusiast Brands, LLC

Printed in China
1 3 5 7 9 10 8 6 4 2

Pictured on the front cover:
American copper, Glenn Traver
Purple coneflower, Dennis Frates/Alamy Stock Photo
Buff-bellied hummingbird, Gail Buquoi

Pictured on the back cover:
Gray catbird, Richard Day/Daybreak Imagery
Monarch butterflies, Mary Carlson
Barred owls, John Gill

(GREAT HORNED OWL); BOB KOTHENBEUTEL (BLACK-CAPPED CHICKADEE)

# CHAPTER 1

# The Joys of Bird-Watching

Enjoy a fresh peek into the world of birding. Read all about avian flight patterns, migration, birdcalls and more. Plus, discover fascinating facts about your favorite backyard visitors, elusive species like owls and other sought-after birds.

DEB POTTS

# up,
## UP AND

A red-tailed hawk glides above an open field, hunting for its next meal.

# AWAY

Whether they're opening for takeoff, spreading wide for a lazy soar or flapping to brake for landing, a bird's wings make flying look almost effortless.

**BY KENN AND KIMBERLY KAUFMAN**

Like other swallows, barn swallows have very long wings relative to their body size.

Yellow-headed blackbird

*T*he Wright Brothers studied bird flight before they designed the first airplane. Now modern aircraft fly higher and faster than any bird, yet no manufactured device matches the graceful movements and mechanics of a bird's wing.

The average bird wing is a remarkably complicated thing. The bone-and-muscle part is relatively small, and most of the visible surface area is composed only of strong feathers. Thanks to the muscles, birds have the ability to constantly change the shape and angle of their wings for masterful control in the air.

It may look as if your favorite birds are simply flapping their wings straight up and down as they fly. But if they did that, they'd never get anywhere. A closer look reveals that their wings reach ahead on the upstroke and push back on the downstroke, propelling the bird forward. The feathers on the outer part of the wing spread apart on the upstroke, letting air through, and flatten into a solid surface on the downstroke so they're pushing down against the air with every flap. If you take a cross-section view, the upper surface is curved and the

A bald eagle uses its strength to push down with its wings and propel itself into the sky.

*Songbirds like the American goldfinch can fly short daily distances and long migration routes, too.*

American goldfinch

lower surface is flat, creating an airfoil like that of an airplane wing. As the bird moves forward, the curved upper surface causes the air to flow faster over the top of the wing, creating lift. So even when the bird glides or soars, the wing shape helps keep it up in the air.

When a bird isn't flying, it folds its wings neatly and tucks them against its body, out of the way. What's more, when the wings are closed, the feathers that are most important for flight are folded under the others, protected against wear and tear as the bird moves around in foliage or grass.

There is tremendous diversity in the shapes of wings, and the differences relate to how the birds use them. A ground-dwelling bird like a northern bobwhite gets around mostly by walking, and only occasionally has to make a quick flight to scurry away from danger. Its wings are very short and rounded, ideal for a rapid escape but not for sustained flight. On the other hand, a barn swallow spends most of the day in the air, swooping about gracefully to catch flying insects. Its wings are longer than its body and sharply pointed.

Between these two extremes are more typical songbirds such as robins and goldfinches. They make many short flights every day, and may fly long distances during migration. Their wings are slightly pointed, and just large enough to fit their active lifestyles.

*Frigatebirds can fly for days or even weeks at a time without landing.*

Magnificent frigatebird

Birds that spend a lot of time soaring over land have long and wide wings. Vultures, eagles and red-tailed hawks are good examples. As the sun warms the land, it creates currents of rising warm air, called thermals. Soaring birds hitch a ride on these thermals, circling up into the sky without any effort.

Large seabirds, however, often have very narrow wings. Albatrosses, such as the black-footed albatross commonly seen off our Pacific Coast, maneuver easily in strong winds with their incredibly long, thin wings. Another narrow-winged seabird, the magnificent frigatebird, soars over the Florida Keys and elsewhere on the Florida coast. Recent research shows frigatebirds can fly for days or even weeks at a time without landing, even sleeping as they soar high above tropical oceans.

The wings of birds that don't take to the air aren't useless, though. An ostrich dashing across the African plains sticks its stubby, fluffy wings out to the side to help balance during high-speed turns. Penguins use theirs as flippers to propel them in powerful, graceful swimming—in effect "flying" underwater.

As birds fly in and out of your backyard, watch for connections between the way they fly and the shape of their wings. And the next time you're in an airplane, thank the birds.

## THE WONDER OF WINGS

They come in a dazzling variety of shapes, but most bird wings have the same basic groups of feathers. The long outermost feathers are the primaries, those on the trailing (back) edge on the inner part of the wing are the secondaries, and those closest to the body on the trailing edge are tertials.

The primaries, secondaries and tertials are collectively called the flight feathers. The bases of all these feathers are covered up by smaller feathers called (naturally enough) the coverts. And a small, separate group of feathers on the leading edge of the wing, the alula, is similar to a human's thumb.

*Tertials*

*Secondaries*

*Coverts*

*Alula*

*Primaries*

**The blue-winged warbler gets its name from the bluish-gray color of its wings.**

# AROUND THE WORLD
## *and Back Again*

**Sandhill cranes
at Bosque del
Apache National
Wildlife Refuge**

*Whether flying north to south or zigzagging between oceans, migrating birds have some spectacular flight patterns.*

**BY KEN KEFFER**

# Look up at the sky!

If it's migration season, you might see geese determinedly winging overhead in a synchronized V-shape. Of course these aren't the only birds that pack their bags for warmer weather. "We humans barely comprehend the scale of bird migration because most migration occurs at night," says nature writer and bird expert Scott Weidensaul. His book about the phenomenon, *Living on the Wind*, was a finalist for a Pulitzer Prize in 2000. Yet despite his vast knowledge on the subject, his sense of wonder is still fresh and contagious.

"The great thing about migration is its ubiquity. Anywhere I find myself during migration season, I'm probably in a patch that is graced by global travelers passing through and connecting the farthest corners of the earth in their journeys," Scott says. Feathered flight is captivating in its own right, but the show really begins when birds crisscross the skies above, traveling thousands of miles. Here are the most spectacular of the bunch.

## ARCTIC TERNS

If bird migrations were marathons, the arctic tern would be the world champion marathoner. These elegant fliers travel upward of 25,000 miles annually on their epic journeys. From Arctic summers in the north to Antarctic summers in the south, their odysseys take them to every ocean. Although it may seem unbelievable that these birds zigzag across the globe, there's a method to the madness. Instead of flying straight north in spring, they follow spiraling patterns to avoid flying into the wind. They spend most of the year at sea but come back to solid land to breed in the northern summer. During this time, arctic terns can be spotted as far south as New England.

Bar-tailed godwit

Arctic tern

## GODWITS

These hefty shorebirds stand well over a foot tall. There are four species of godwits: bar-tailed, Hudsonian, marbled and black-tailed. The Hudsonian godwit is named for its Hudson Bay breeding grounds, and the marbled godwit's name reflects its spotted feathers. Both marbled and Hudsonian godwits can be seen moving between their summer and winter ranges, but the prize for the longest flight without a layover goes to the bar-tailed godwits. These birds fly for a week from western Alaska to New Zealand and Australia without stopping. "I have a hard time wrapping my head around that," Scott says. "No refueling, no resting, no drinking, but continual powered flight for some 7,200 miles across the Pacific Ocean."

Arctic terns travel more than *25,000 miles* on their heroic annual journeys.

**DID YOU KNOW?**
A 17th-century minister and scientist named Charles Morton tried to explain migration with his odd theory that birds went to the moon and back, flying 125 mph to reach their out-of-this-world destination in 60 days.

## RED KNOTS

When it comes to eating on the go, red knots are professionals with a highly specialized migration strategy. The annual journey of this shorebird species coincides with the spring breeding of horseshoe crabs on the East Coast, and thousands of red knots take full advantage of the May buffet. Red knots are found worldwide, but among those that migrate through eastern North America, up to 90 percent may be present on the beaches of Delaware Bay at once. "Delaware Bay provides stopover habitat to more than just the red knot. Semipalmated sandpipers, ruddy turnstones, sanderlings and even laughing gulls are all eating the horseshoe crab eggs," says David La Puma, director of the Cape May Bird Observatory. Birds can be spotted chowing down throughout the day, but high tide in the evening is an especially busy time.

Tree swallows

## RUBY-THROATED HUMMINGBIRDS

As the weather starts to grow colder, migrating birds head to warmer climates in the south where food is plentiful. Because flying over a large body of water means no stopping to rest, the Gulf of Mexico is a very challenging barrier for many eastern birds. Some species go thousands of miles out of their way to fly around the Gulf, but some ruby-throated hummingbirds fly straight over it to Central America. It takes ruby throats about 18 hours to make the journey, a lot faster than if they had taken a detour along the coast. Before they take off on their solitary flights, they fuel up and put on weight, and if they get tired en route, they sometimes rest on boats. You might spot some of these travelers if you visit the Gulf Coast in September or March, and you won't see them until May in the northern states and Canada.

Ruby-throated hummingbird

## PURPLE MARTINS AND TREE SWALLOWS

Although most birds are nocturnal migrants, a few species travel during the day. Every fall, tree swallows and purple martins pile up in the New Jersey marshes of Cape May on their southbound flights. "Martins are strictly insectivorous, and they move out in early fall," David says. "Tree swallows can feed on myrtle berries and migrate a bit later." If you're in the area during fall migration, watch for purple martins, swallows, swifts, and other daytime migrants such as cranes, gulls, pelicans and jays.

Sandhill cranes

Cooper's hawk

## HAWKS

Raptors prefer daylight for migration, too. If wind conditions are good, a breathtaking cast of hawks can be spotted in a single day. "With hawk-watching, you wind up with a tight-knit community of folks who hang out together year after year, filling long hours of hawk-watching with stories and food," Scott says. "I started hawk-watching when I was 12 and immediately felt as though I'd found my tribe. I still feel that way."

Nebraska's Platte River
hosts an epic
migratory gathering of

## *600,000*

sandhill cranes.

Bear River
Migratory Bird
Refuge

### SANDHILL CRANES

According to Scott, every birder in America
should pencil in a visit to Nebraska in
March to witness one of the greatest wildlife
spectacles in the world. "Waves of waterfowl
surge up through Nebraska's Rainwater Basin,
ending in the absolute epic gathering of
600,000 sandhill cranes on the Platte River,"
he says. "The sight is amazing, and if the
sound of all those cranes raising the roof with
their trumpets at daybreak doesn't give you
goose bumps, then you need to check yourself
for a pulse."

## DESTINATION MIGRATION

*Migration plays out in backyards
across the continent, but some
spectacular shows are best seen
when you take to the road.*

### Great Salt Lake, Utah

This large inland salt lake is a migration
magnet for waterfowl. Antelope Island State
Park puts you in the middle of the action,
while nearby Bear River Migratory Bird
Refuge sees its peak duck migration in March,
with shorebirds flying through in April.

### Kiptopeke State Park, Virginia

Along the southern tip of the Delmarva
Peninsula, birds concentrate at Kiptopeke
State Park. As at Cape May in the north,
migration here is even better in the fall
than in spring. Look for warblers, flycatchers
and vireos.

### Dauphin Island, Alabama

After crossing the Gulf of Mexico, birds often
touch down at the first sight of land. There
are numerous hot spots from the Texas coast
to the Florida Panhandle. On Dauphin Island,
the Audubon Bird Sanctuary boasts 3 miles
of National Recreation Trail and makes a
prime destination for birds and birders alike.

A chickadee's most common call sounds as if it is saying its own name, *chickadee-dee-dee.*

A yellow warbler midsong

# Tune In to Bird Songs

*Whether protecting their territory or finding a partner, birds create fascinating music for all kinds of reasons.* BY KENN AND KIMBERLY KAUFMAN

From lovely melodies to raucous squawks, birds make all sorts of interesting sounds. Of course they aren't making that variety of sounds just to entertain you; they have more practical reasons for belting their hearts out. Birds use songs and calls to communicate with other birds, particularly their own kind, and when you dig deeper, the reasons get even more complex.

A few species, like turkey vultures, are almost always silent, but most birds are chatterboxes and have several different calls. This is especially true for birds that live in flocks for part of the year, such as chickadees.

Black-capped chickadees have at least 15 distinct calls that they use in various situations. If their flock is foraging in treetops, they make short, light "contact" calls and a louder note when the flock is ready to move on. Chickadees make various alarm calls when danger is near. Rival males have aggressive calls they use when they're about to have a showdown. Members of a mated pair have several noises they use to communicate with each other when near the nest, and young chickadees make food-begging and distress calls.

Chestnut-sided warblers spend their winters in Central America, often joining up with flocks of tropical birds.

Male Baltimore orioles sing to defend territory or lure a mate.

Some types of alarm notes are recognized by other birds, too, not just the species that makes them. When a mixed flock of different species is moving through the forest and one member spots an approaching hawk or owl, it pays for every bird in the flock to recognize the alarm call.

While calls typically consist of a single note, bird songs tend to be more complicated and have a very distinct purpose. The songs can be beautiful, like those of the wood thrush or hermit thrush, but that's not always the case. The yellow-headed blackbird, for example, has a rough nasal snarl for a song. Although it's not the prettiest song out there, that harsh performance works just as well as any of the other melodious offerings from different bird species.

It's primarily the male birds that sing, mostly in the breeding season, and they use their songs to announce a territory claim. If you see a male robin or oriole singing away, he's warning other males that this plot of ground is already taken and to stay off his turf. His song can also serve to attract a female or to help the male stay in touch with his mate, but territorial defense seems to be the main motivation to sing.

However, the male in some species of warblers has two song types: one for chasing away other males and the other for keeping in contact with his mate.

And there are some bird species, especially in the tropics, in which the males and females even sing duets. All of these different sounds add variety to nature's soundtrack.

## VOICE LESSONS

Birds generally are born knowing how to make the right callnotes by instinct, but many have to learn their songs by listening to adults of their own kind. For that reason, some species (like white-crowned sparrows) have song "dialects" that vary from one place to another, while the calls tend to be the same within every location.

Brown thrashers have a huge repertoire of songs copied from other bird species.

repeat

*Just like your favorite cover band, these copycat birds belt out songs that aren't their own.*

**BY KEN KEFFER**

# after me

# b irds are known for their

homemade music, but not all of their tunes are original. Mimics are the cover artists of the bird world, borrowing tunes from other birds to use as their own. Some species— mockingbirds, thrashers and catbirds—may sing more than a hundred different phrases. These slim birds all have distinctive long tails and usually have plumage in earthy tones, like gray and brown. Here's everything you need to know about locating and luring these sweet pretenders.

## HOT SPOT

On your next Texas adventure, try Big Bend National Park. Paddle down the Rio Grande and see if you can spot mimic species like curve-billed thrashers and plenty of other species, like crissals and green kingfishers.

The Southwest's arid climate is perfect for curve-billed thrashers, a species that can produce more than 1,000 snippets of stolen song.

# Thrashers

### ON TOUR

The U.S. Southwest, Mexico and the Caribbean islands are thrasher hot spots. The curve-billed is the most common in the southwestern states, while a look-alike species, Bendire's thrasher, has a more restricted range centered on Arizona and western Mexico. The California thrasher prefers the brushy chaparral hills of its namesake state, while the sage thrasher is found in the western flats from southern Canada to northern Mexico. Most have long down-curved bills, although the two most widespread, the brown and the sage thrashers, have straighter bills.

### BEHIND THE MUSIC

The brown thrasher stands out because it usually repeats each phrase twice. Other mimics will repeat things, but consistently doing them twice is a brown thrasher specialty.

### HOST A BACKYARD CONCERT

Entice thrashers into your backyard with thick cover. To do this, build a brush pile and sprinkle some seeds nearby. Thrashers usually scamper across the ground, flinging leaf litter in search of invertebrate snacks. Grow a thick hedgerow of native shrubs to provide good shelter for many kinds of critters. Thrashes love fruits and berries, too. Juniper, sage, mesquite and chaparral shrub are favorite haunts for thrashers in the West, and curve-billed thrashers particularly love cholla cactus, which is their preferred nesting site.

# Mockingbirds

## ON TOUR

Northern mockingbirds are found in parks and backyards throughout the southern and central United States, but they've been known to wander northward, even as far north as the Bering Sea region of Alaska. They're the only mockingbird regularly found in the United States, but 13 species live throughout Central and South America. A handful of species are on the Galapagos Islands, observations of which helped shape Charles Darwin's thoughts on evolution.

## BEHIND THE MUSIC

Thanks to their incessant singing, northern mockingbirds are quite conspicuous. Their song is a series of short phrases repeated over and over, usually in sets of three or more. New phrases, as many as 200, are added to their repertoire throughout their lifetimes. Their scientific name, *Mimus polyglottos*, translates to "mimic with many tongues." This species mimics not only other birds but also noises like cellphones, car alarms and the whistles of passing trains.

## HOST A BACKYARD CONCERT

Encourage mockingbirds with perches and suet feeders. Sometimes mockingbirds flash their white wing patches, either as a display or as a way to startle up one of their favorite summer treats: insects. During fall and winter, mockingbirds camp out in fruit trees gorging on the ripe harvests, but you can offer them any fruits and berries in feeders year-round.

The incessant mimicking of other birds and man-made sounds makes northern mockingbirds difficult to ignore.

Meow! Gray catbirds are named after their call, which sounds like a cat's.

# Catbirds

## ON TOUR

While the gray catbird is absent from the Southwest and much of the West Coast, it's widespread throughout the rest of the country. Several unrelated species of catbirds are found in the world, like the green catbird of Australia and the white-eared catbird of New Guinea, but none of the others is a mimic like the gray catbird.

## BEHIND THE MUSIC

Although they have well-defined rictal bristles (the bird version of whiskers), gray catbirds are actually named after their meowing callnotes. Catbirds often meow from thick cover, but they venture out into open areas, especially to feed. The least accomplished of mimics, they typically sing a series of disjointed notes, squeaks and whines. Catbirds don't often repeat phrases, either. However, individuals do add phrases they've picked up from birds, other animals or man-made sound sources, inserting them around the catbird gibberish.

## HOST A BACKYARD CONCERT

Gray catbirds are suckers for sweets, and they love backyard fruit feeders that include orange slices and grape jelly. Like thrashers, catbirds use brush piles, but another favorite is thickets of dogwood. These shrubs provide good cover, and the berries are an excellent meal.

# SONGSTERS
## *in the* SKY

A male bobolink
flies low before
bursting into song.

*Look up if you hear music overhead!
Birds such as sandpipers and larks
sing on the wing—their high-flying
concerts are sure to impress.*

**BY KENN AND KIMBERLY KAUFMAN**

Pectoral
sandpiper

An American golden-
plover pauses on the
Arctic tundra between
song-flight displays.

Birdsongs may simply be pretty outdoor melodies to humans, but for birds, there are practical uses behind the music. Male birds mainly sing to announce their claim to a territory and to attract a mate. They need to be heard, so they often sit up on a prominent, high perch to deliver their serenades. For example, a male cardinal may take to the top of a tall tree to sing his song, and a male song sparrow may fly up to the tallest nearby bush to sing after hunting for food on the ground.

But if there aren't any towering shrubs or trees nearby, there's always the highest perch of all: the sky. Many birds that live in wide-open country make that choice, pouring out their songs while fluttering through the heavens above their patch of territory on the ground.

One of the most widespread flight-singers is the horned lark. This common bird, named for the tiny feather-tuft "horns" on its head, is found coast to coast but is easy to overlook. It spends most of its time on flat, open ground, such as plowed fields, pastures, short-grass prairies, southwestern deserts or Arctic tundra. At the start of the nesting season in early spring, the male horned lark begins his performance. He flies silently up and up to a towering height,

Horned lark

often more than 500 feet above the ground. Then he faces into the breeze, spreads his wings and tail wide, and sings a musical, tinkling song. He may sing over and over, staying aloft for up to 10 minutes before abruptly swooping back down to the ground.

Many shorebirds, including plovers and sandpipers, migrate to the Arctic tundra in summer to nest and raise their young. The tundra has no tall trees, so many of these shorebirds, as well as other Arctic birds, perform flight songs. The American golden-plover flies in wide circles, with slow, deep wingbeats, singing a series of mellow whistles. An odd flight display is performed by the

Chestnut-collared longspur

male pectoral sandpiper, who puffs out his chest until he almost looks as round as a basketball, then flies in circles while making a deep, hollow hooting sound.

The Great Plains, which is the prairie heartland of North America, has many flight-singers. Some of them are small songbirds, such as the lark bunting, Sprague's pipit and chestnut-collared longspur. One of the most beautiful songs is the breathy whistle of the upland sandpiper. This graceful "shorebird" that lives far from the shore is a strong flier. It migrates to South America and back every year. Once in its breeding grounds, it sings from the tops of fence posts and other raised perches, but usually floats

The Wilson's snipe forages for food in shallow water.

Eurasian skylark

on the wing high above the prairies to deliver its ghostly, whistled song.

Another member of the sandpiper family that sings on the wing is the American woodcock. This secretive bird hides in woodlands during the day, but at dusk during the nesting season, the male woodcock flies over wet fields, making a chirping, twittering sound. However, only the chirping sounds are vocally made. The twittering is created by wind rushing through the narrow outermost feathers of his wings.

A bird related to the woodcock, the Wilson's snipe, also has a surprising way of making music. As the male snipe zooms through the sky over his nesting territory, he makes a rippling, hollow bleating sound, or "winnowing." The sound is created by the narrow outermost feathers of the tail, which vibrate rapidly as the snipe swoops and dives through the air.

Not all flight-singing birds go high overhead, though. The male bobolink sings while flying in a circle over the meadows, but often he's only a few yards above the top of the grass. He has such a striking color pattern that he may fly so low partly to show it off. The impact would be lost if he were high up in the sky. So he flutters and sings in plain sight, delighting the humans who get to watch.

Practically every location in North America has at least a few kinds of birds that sing while in flight. Watch and listen for them when you visit open country, and you may be treated to a most impressive and acrobatic aerial concert.

## THE MOST FAMOUS SKY-SINGER OF THEM ALL

"Hail to thee, blithe Spirit!" That's the first line of *To a Skylark*, written by British poet Percy Bysshe Shelley in 1820. Skylarks are popular birds in England, where they sing while fluttering high over farms and fields.

Shelley wasn't the first poet to write about skylarks. Shakespeare mentioned the species more than once, most notably in the play *Romeo and Juliet*.

Skylarks aren't native to North America, but they have been introduced in Hawaii and in farm country around Victoria, British Columbia. Larks from Asia also sometimes wander into Alaska.

## HOT SPOT

*Head to North Dakota's national wildlife refuges for an up-close look at a few of these sky-singers.* In late spring and early summer, the Des Lacs, Lostwood and Upper Souris refuges play host to sky-singers, like upland sandpipers, Wilson's snipes, horned larks, bobolinks and Sprague's pipits.

*Meet Your*
# Nocturnal Neighbors

*Step outside after dark and watch your backyard come to life as owls swoop through the night skies.* **BY KEN KEFFER**

# W

hen the sun goes down and the streetlights turn on, most owls' days are just getting started. These mysterious birds like to keep a low profile, so although there's probably at least one living in your neighborhood, chances are you've never seen it.

Owls are among the most specialized and highly adapted bird groups. With their keen vision and hearing, they hunt at night for small prey (think mice, voles and toads). Fringed feathers ensure silent flight, while sharp beaks and talons allow them to grasp and eat their prey.

These birds rest during the day, and they can be difficult to see due to their camouflaged feathers. One of the best ways to spot an owl is to pay close attention to other birds, such as crows and jays. These smaller birds mob an owl by harassing it with loud calls and betraying its hiding spot in the process. The jury is still out on why birds do this, but one theory is that it is an attempt to drive the owl, a predator, away from the area.

The next time you suspect an owl may have moved in down the street, check out this roundup of the most common owl varieties in North America.

**THE NO. 1 PLACE** to see burrowing owls is in Cape Coral, Florida. You are bound to see at least a few of the over 1,000 nesting pairs during a visit.

## BURROWING OWLS

An oddity in the owl world, burrowing owls are among the few species to nest underground. The southern Florida populations dig their own chambers, while burrowing owls in the Southwest rely on holes dug by other animals, including prairie dogs, badgers and ground squirrels. Look for burrowing owls perched on fence posts or other low perches, swiveling their heads from side to side.

## BARN OWLS

Although barn owls are found worldwide, there's no one place where they're particularly abundant. There are over 40 different races of barn owls, but the North American variety is the largest and makes up approximately 9 percent of the world's barn owl population. True to their name, barn owls nest and roost in barns, silos and other human-made structures. They can also be found living in large nest boxes, tree cavities and caves. These skilled rodent-slayers have heart-shaped faces and are ghostly white with warm brown coloration on their backs and wings.

Barn owl

Barred owl

## BARRED OWLS

*Who cooks for you? Who cooks for you allll?* This is the eerie-sounding call of the barred owl, heard throughout forests in the eastern United States, southern Canada and increasingly the Pacific Northwest. The expansion of barred owls into Washington and Oregon is a threat to spotted owls, because the larger and more aggressive barred owls displace the spotted species. Meanwhile, barred owls have a threat of their own to fear, as nearby great horned owls are among their major predators.

Although barred owls have moved into other states, these birds are homebodies. They don't migrate, and of 158 banded barred owls who were found later, none had moved farther than 6 miles away.

**OWL ON THE PROWL**
Short-eared owls fly low while hunting.

### EARED OWLS

Long-eared owls are slim doppelgängers of great horned owls. But take a closer look at their markings. Intersecting vertical and horizontal barring creates a checkerboard-like pattern on their chests, while great horneds only have horizontal barring. Long-eareds roost in thick foliage near open areas where they hunt for prey, which include voles, mice and young rabbits. Long-eared owls don't typically construct their own nests, instead moving into abandoned ones built by other birds such as ravens, crows and hawks.

Short-eared owls live in open areas, preferring to hunt and roost in grasslands, marshes and tundra. As you might have guessed from their name, their "ears" are so short, they are difficult to see at all. One of the most common owl species in the United States, the short-eared is also one of the few owl species that build their nests themselves. The female of a short-eared pair scrapes a bowl-shaped nest into the ground and lines it with materials like grass and soft feathers.

### GREAT HORNED OWLS

Equally comfortable nesting in the cactuses of the Desert Southwest as in the forests of the far north, the great horned is one of the most widespread owl species in North America. Great horned owls are tough, taking down other large predators like ospreys and falcons with their strong talons. These birds of prey have one of the most diverse diets among owl species and are capable of eating porcupines, scorpions, bats, skunks and even other owls. They are early-season nesters and have been known to take over prefab nests built by other birds. Despite their name, these owls don't actually have horns—the two telltale points at the tops of their heads are feather tufts.

Screech owl

### SCREECH-OWLS

There are three species of screech-owls in the United States: eastern in the East, western in the West and whiskered along the southern borders of Arizona and New Mexico. Screech-owls are cavity-nesters and are enticed into wooded backyards with nest boxes. Location aside, one of the best ways to distinguish between them is by their calls. Eastern screech-owls can be heard giving their best whinnying horse impersonations. Western and whiskered screech-owls call out with hoots, toots and doots. Screech-owls eat a variety of things, from insects to small mammals.

# Extreme Owls

- **LARGEST**
Great gray owls can reach up to 2½ feet in length.

- **HEAVIEST**
Snowy owls weigh somewhere between 3 and 5 pounds.

- **SMALLEST**
Elf owls are sparrow-sized at just 5½ inches long, and they weigh about as much as a golf ball.

Great horned owl

# scratching up a storm

*Look down! That noise under your shrubs is a shy, ground-feeding towhee in search of its next meal.*

**BY KENN AND KIMBERLY KAUFMAN**

An eastern towhee strikes a perfect pose in a flowering crabapple tree.

W hen dry leaves rustle beneath your shrubs, you may think it's a fidgety squirrel at first, but look closer. If you hear an odd, sharp call through the noise, a towhee may be responsible for the racket. Crouch down low and peer through the dense branches to catch a glimpse of this secretive visitor.

A little larger than their sparrow relatives, towhees spend a lot of time on the hunt for seeds and insects by scratching at dry leaf litter on the ground. You might assume that a bird stands on one foot and scratches with the other, but towhees have their own approach: They jump in the air and kick backward with both feet, sending dry leaves flying and exposing their favorite foods.

Anywhere in the eastern half of the U.S., scratching sounds that come from under dense thickets could reveal the presence of an eastern towhee. Males of this species are mostly black and white while females are mostly brown and white, but they both show a wide stripe of reddish brown, or rufous, along the side of the body.

Eastern types thrive in second-growth woods, overgrown fields or tall forest edges, but they show up in backyards that have low, dense bushes. Listen for their sharp, ringing call, which sounds like *chewink* (or, if you use your imagination, *towhee*). Their song is a musical *drink-your-tea*.

The western half of the country is the spotted towhee's territory. It looks a lot like its eastern cousin and chooses similar habitats, but it has extra white spots on its back. Another difference is the calls and songs. Those of western towhees are much more variable.

Two of the plainest brown birds in North America are the canyon towhee of the Southwest and the California towhee of California and Oregon. These two were once considered one species, called brown towhee, but their voices are completely different. What they lack in bright colors they make up for with personality. They live in pairs year-round, and the male and female both defend their nesting territory, loudly chasing away other towhees. And although the male does most of the actual singing, both members of the pair sing squealing, chattering duets together several times a day.

California towhees live near the Pacific coast in gardens, where they scurry across patios and bustle under hedges. Canyon towhees tend to live in the more wild country of foothills and canyons, but they come into the suburbs of some Southwestern cities, like Albuquerque. There's a third relative, called Abert's towhee, with a very limited range. It lives along rivers and streams in Arizona and southeastern California, barely extending into the edges of other nearby states.

Along wild rivers it can be very shy and hard to see. But in recent years some Abert's towhees have adapted to living around people, and they have become common garden birds in some parts of Phoenix and Yuma, Arizona.

Just a little smaller than other towhees, the green-tailed towhee is mostly a western bird. It spends the summer in mountain forests, and for the winter it migrates to dense thickets along rivers and streams in the Southwest. As its name suggests, it has yellow-green on the tail, wings and back. But you're more likely to notice its rusty-red forehead—especially since it often raises those forehead feathers in a perky crest. The most common callnote is a soft *mew* that sounds like a kitten in the shrubbery.

## HOT SPOT

*During your next visit to the Grand Canyon State, add Saguaro National Park to your itinerary. Canyon towhees are common, spotted and Abert's are present year-round, and green-tailed ones visit during migration and winter. With luck, you could pick up four towhee species.*

Although they're cousins, a green-tailed towhee (previous page) looks remarkably different from this spotted towhee.

California towhees eat seeds from many types of grasses and herbs, like this tickseed.

Even though the green-tailed towhee is typical of the West, it occasionally wanders far eastward and has even shown up at feeders on the Atlantic coast. Spotted towhees also stray east at times, and the eastern towhee occasionally drifts out west. So the next time you hear mysterious rustling coming from your shrubs, see if a towhee chose to visit your yard.

Here an Abert's towhee perches in the Sonoran Desert.

# 3 Easy Ways to Attract Towhees

**1** **HABITAT.** Keep shrub branches low and allow dry leaves to accumulate under them.

**2** **FOOD.** Serve quality seed, like white proso millet. But don't be surprised if towhees prefer to forage on the ground.

**3** **WATER.** Put out a ground-level birdbath with a dripper or source of moving water.

# Harbingers of Spring

Aawnk-ah-rrreeee! *Red-winged blackbirds are back! Get to know these scarlet-spotted fliers.* **BY CHRISTINA CRAIG**

**2**

**BEHAVIOR TO WATCH FOR**
*There are two reasons males flash their scarlet field marks, hunch their shoulders forward, and spread their tails: to mark their territory or to impress a potential mate.*

**14** *Red-winged blackbirds leave the nest 11 to 14 days after birth.*

**800** True snowbirds, red-winged blackbirds travel as many as 800 miles south for the winter.

**1766** *Carolus Linnaeus, a Swedish scientist, gave the red-wing its scientific name,* Agelaius phoeniceus, *in 1766. The name comes from the Greek words for flocking and red.*

**3** *Females often lay three or four pale blue-green eggs, accented with black, brown and purple markings.*

**40** The species, one of the most abundant in all of North America, has experienced a decrease in population over the past 40 years.

**15** *Male red-winged blackbirds can't commit. They juggle as many as 15 female mates.*

Female red-winged blackbird

**DADDY DUTY**
A male purple martin with his lighter-colored offspring. Both the males and females choose a home and build the nest.

# Return of the Martins

*Purple-hued swallows arrive just in time to select a new home.* **BY SHERYL DEVORE**

An estimated 1 million purple martin landlords listen each spring for the chortling call of their summer tenants reappearing from the south and announcing that birdhouses across the country will be filled with adults ready to raise their young.

Historically, purple martins nested in natural tree hollows, old woodpecker holes, and cliff crevices near water throughout most of the U.S. The birds continue to do so in the West, especially in saguaro cacti, but in the eastern half, martins nest almost exclusively in man-made boxes. Native Americans began the tradition thousands of years ago when they found that a hollow gourd placed in a tree was attractive to breeding bird pairs. Houses made by humans are now essential to the martins' survival.

Males are black all over with bluish-purple reflections; the females are blackish from above and have sooty gray underparts; and young birds look like females but have whiter bellies. All martins have pointed wings and forked tails.

That distinctive tail helps them catch flying insects, like dragonflies, as they fly about 100 to 200 feet in the air. Martins can often be heard calling as they glide above forested areas in an attempt to attract some younger adults to the colony. These birds rarely land on the ground and even drink water while in flight.

The first to arrive in spring are often called scouts, but that's a misnomer. As with many species that breed in North America but migrate to and from the tropics, the first to return are the older males on their way to claim last year's nesting sites. Females and younger birds arrive later. In the Midwest, the northern part of the range, martins start to arrive as early as March. Then the search for the perfect home begins.

Nests typically consist of grasses and twigs, with fresh green leaves added throughout the season. The female incubates three to six white eggs for 15 to 16 days. Both adults raise and feed the young, which fledge in about 30 days and then beg their parents for food for several more weeks.

Being a purple martin landlord takes time and commitment. In summer, boxes must be kept free of non-native house sparrows; in late fall, boxes must be cleaned and closed. But it's all worth the effort: Hosting purple martins means you'll get to enjoy these feathered good neighbors during spring and summer before they fly the coop in fall.

**REAL TALK**

"Martin houses are a hub of activity. It's fascinating to watch purple martins come and go. I love to watch for the youngsters poking their heads out of the boxes."
**Ken Keffer**, naturalist

**BE THE BEST LANDLORD**
Purple martins like to nest in colonies. Whether you choose gourd houses or an apartment-style setup, offer six to 12 cavities. Place the birdhouse in an open area that is 40 to 60 feet from trees and 12 to 18 feet high. Learn more at *purplemartin.org*

**HOST SEVERAL**
pairs with a 12-room convertible martin house from *plowhearth.com*

**TAKE IT ALL IN** Nothing says spring quite like a picturesque American robin in a flowering crabapple tree.

# Rockin' Robin

*Meet the orange-breasted early bird that greets spring with a song.* **BY SHERYL DEVORE**

When you hear an American robin's light, musical *cheerily, cheerio*, it means spring is at your doorstep. As the ground thaws and worms break through the surface, robins become more active and present in your backyard. But you can find this member of the thrush family even when it's snowing, gobbling up berries from shrubs and trees. Occasionally, you may notice a robin that looks slightly uncoordinated. That's because it gorged itself on overripe berries and is a bit tipsy!

Robins are common sights in backyards throughout most of North America and willingly nest in planters, on windowsills, and in other nooks and crannies around a building. In spring, look for pairs hopping around your yard. Both males and females have yellow bills and orange breasts, but the male's head is usually darker than the female's. Robins in the eastern part of the United States show white spots in the outer corners of their tails while in flight.

In a robin couple, the female builds the cuplike nest with mud as its foundation and lines it with grasses, twigs and other plant material. She typically lays four bright blue eggs and incubates them for about two weeks. Both parents feed the young, which have dark-spotted breasts rather than red ones. Robins can raise three or more broods a year, especially in the southern part of the United States.

As the weather cools into fall, robins gather in flocks, sometimes up to tens of thousands, to roost together at night. They also make small migratory movements to find food. Robins eat berries year-round, so lure them to your yard with trees that hold fruit in winter such as chokecherry, hawthorn and dogwood. Watch for these classic birds in your yard, no matter what the weather is like.

**ROBIN'S EGG BLUE**
It became an iconic color thanks to Tiffany & Co.'s famous jewelry boxes. Its trademarked, custom Pantone shade is No. 1837, the year the company was founded.

> A wish made upon seeing the first robin in spring will come true—but only if you complete the wish before the robin flies away.
>
> IRISH SUPERSTITION

**WORMS RULE!**
The next time you observe an American robin in your yard, notice how they curiously tilt their heads. They do this to listen for juicy worms. Robins use both visual and auditory clues to hunt down their favorite slimy snack.

# Glad You Asked!

*Bird and garden pros tackle the toughest backyard questions.*

**Q** When a brown-colored thrush visited my platform feeder, it gobbled up the food. In it was a mix including berries, nuts, sunflower seeds, milo, millet and suet cake. The bird didn't touch the suet. What should I serve in the feeder to lure this bird back?

**Kirk Klag** TIMKEN, KANSAS

**KENN AND KIMBERLY:** Thrushes aren't common visitors to feeders because they don't eat seeds. Their typical diet is mostly insects and berries. Since your mix included berries, it was probably going for those. If you want to attract thrushes and other birds that don't typically visit feeders, add a water feature with moving water. Even a small fountain or dripper can work like a charm if it has an area large and flat enough for birds to splash in. For a long-term plan, consider planting native fruiting trees, shrubs and vines. Dogwood, serviceberry, elderberry and wild grape are among our favorites for attracting thrushes.

Swainson's thrush

To ID a mystery bird such as this house sparrow, look at the size and shape of the beak.

**Q** My neighbor thinks this is a female goldfinch, but my husband says it's a female junco. What do you think?

**Patrice Iacovoni** WATERFORD, MICHIGAN

**KENN AND KIMBERLY:** One of the trickiest birds in North America, often overlooked or misidentified, is the female house sparrow. She has some strong stripes on the back, but from this front view she looks absolutely plain, with no markings at all. And this one looks a little odd because her feathers are fluffed up against the cold. To identify this bird, we look at the size and shape of the bill, the shape of the tail, the slight pale area above and behind the eye, the overall dusty color, and the lack of actual markings.

**Q** Should I clean out my nesting boxes after every brood is raised?

**John Lentz** GOOSE CREEK, SOUTH CAROLINA

**KENN AND KIMBERLY:** To help keep your birdhouses clean and free from diseases and parasites, it's a very good practice to clean the boxes between each brood. Clearing out the old nest means that the adults can't build on top of it, thus protecting the young from raccoons and other predators that can reach into the box. You don't need any special tools or products to clean house. A wide paint scraper works well for removing the nest material and for scraping any debris off the bottom of the box. It's a good idea to wear gloves, and consider a protective mask to safeguard against inhaling dust and debris.

**Q** How do I discourage bees and wasps from building nests in my birdhouses? **Toby Fencl** MILL CITY, OREGON

**KENN AND KIMBERLY:** To dissuade them, plug the entrance hole until just before the breeding season. Paper wasps build a hanging nest that they attach to the roof of the box. Some nest-box keepers have had success discouraging this by rubbing bar soap on the inside of the roof. The slippery surface prevents the wasps from attaching a nest. Never use pesticides, because the residual effect can be harmful to birds.

**Q** A cardinal and his mate continually fly into my windows. I've tried covering the windows, putting stickers on them and setting out a plastic owl—and nothing seems to work. What can I do?

**Laurien Jeffers** BUMPASS, VIRGINIA

**KENN AND KIMBERLY:** During the breeding season, birds become more territorial and aggressive, especially males. When they see their reflection in a window or mirror, they think it's a rival and may fixate on trying to force the "other bird" out of their territory. They'll keep going as long as they can see the reflection, even between stickers or behind a screen. Rubbing soap on the outside of the window may eliminate the reflection, but if you've exhausted all options, you might have to just be patient until the birds' hormones simmer down.

**SAFETY FIRST!** *If you discover an active bees' or wasps' nest in one of your empty birdhouses, do not attempt to remove it. It's best to leave it be, and wait for cooler temperatures in fall when the insects are less active and less aggressive.*

**Q** I saw this goose in a group of Canada geese and noticed that it was different. What kind is it? **John Yinger** COLUMBUS, OHIO

**KENN AND KIMBERLY:** Interesting goose! It looks like a hybrid—a cross between a Canada goose and a domestic greylag goose. This kind of thing happens occasionally, because geese are not always very picky in mating season. Canada geese are often involved in these mixed pairings, but then the trick is to figure out the identity of the other parent. For the bird in your photo, the overall body color, large pinkish bill and heavy rear end all suggest that a domestic greylag was the other member of the pair.

**Q** I spotted this downy woodpecker on the side of my sugar maple tree. It had its head turned and tucked into its wings as if it was sleeping. What was it doing? **Larry Barger** HAMILTON, OHIO

**KENN AND KIMBERLY:** The bird appears to be taking a short nap. When downy woodpeckers go to sleep for the night, they usually escape to a tree cavity. But sometimes, even midday, a woodpecker may fall asleep for a short time while clinging to a tree trunk. It does this by bracing against the tree with stiff tail feathers and locking its toes onto the bark.

**Q** I've struggled to find this bird in my guidebooks. What is it?

**Charis Adkins** HOUSTON, TEXAS

**KENN AND KIMBERLY:** What a unique individual! It's a male house finch that's having strange issues with his coloration. The amount of red on the head, throat and chest varies a lot when it comes to male house finches. On this one, the color extends far down on the underparts, but much of the red has been replaced by yellow. The bird may have been stressed or eating a poor diet the last time he molted his feathers, which made some grow in yellow instead of red. But that doesn't mean he's unhealthy; he's just one of a kind.

**Q** I scrub the algae off my cement birdbath about every three days. Is there a way to eliminate or reduce the algae that is safe for birds?

**Lorraine Atwood** VICTOR, NEW YORK

**KENN AND KIMBERLY:** Unfortunately, we haven't found a solution better than scrubbing the birdbaths every few days—more often in hot weather. A stiff wire brush makes the process easier. The growth of algae may slow if the water is moving, so add a dripper or small fountain. Even without algae, it's important to replace the water frequently, because otherwise your birdbath may become a breeding ground for mosquitoes.

# Sweet Tweets

*From warblers to woodpeckers, immerse yourself in the stories behind these candid and colorful bird photos.*

I monitor the bluebird boxes at Mosquito Hill Nature Center near New London, Wisconsin. The boxes provide me with plenty of opportunities to find and photograph all of our feathered visitors. This male prothonotary warbler was singing for a mate. I never did see a female, but his song was so lovely it should have attracted many.
**Deb Potts**
WEYAUWEGA, WISCONSIN

**PROTHONOTARY WARBLERS** may choose to nest in a birdhouse in your yard, especially if there are swampy woods nearby. During breeding season, look for these sweet-faced birds snapping their bills at intruders.

**Wood ducks** are very shy waterfowl. I spent many days in chilly, early-spring water with these ducks before they eventually warmed to my presence and gave me some fantastic photo opportunities.
**Harry Collins**
HELLERTOWN, PENNSYLVANIA

**It was a bitterly** cold winter, but for the first time, we had eastern bluebirds in our yard. After they got a drink from the heated birdbath, they flew to one of our trees. Initially they were spread out across the branch, but inch by inch shuffled toward each other until they were huddled together for warmth.
**Steve Trupiano**
O'FALLON, MISSOURI

**MYTH** If a bird uses a heated birdbath during below-freezing temperatures, the bird will freeze.

**FACT** Birds do appreciate a drink from a heated birdbath, but if the temperature is below freezing, they know better than to hop all the way in.

Eastern bluebird
Grand prize winner in our Backyard Photo Contest
**PHOTO BY JIM RIDLEY**

Brown-headed nuthatch
Finalist in our Backyard Photo Contest
**PHOTO BY MARTIN BOZONE**

American goldfinch
Finalist in our Backyard Photo Contest
**PHOTO BY LAMONT KRAFT**

# CHAPTER 2

# Amazing Hummingbirds

Sit back and relax as these energetic little hummers entertain you over the next several pages. Always full of life, beauty and sheer delight, hummingbirds have ingrained themselves in the hearts of birders from coast to coast. See why with these stories!

SALLY RAE KIMMEL

# The Fabulous 14!

Every hummingbird is a mini marvel. More than 350 species of the little gems buzz around the American tropics, and at least 20 of those have been seen north of the Mexican border. Although a few of the hummingbird species are rare visitors, 14 of them nest in the United States every year. Get to know these colorful characters. **BY KENN AND KIMBERLY KAUFMAN**

### THE TROPICAL TEXAN
#### Buff-bellied
Down in southern Texas, this medium-large hummingbird is seen all year, and it sometimes wanders along the Gulf Coast. Males and females look almost the same: apple green on the back, throat and chest; pale buff on the belly; and rusty red on the tail.

## THE DARK KNIGHT
### *Magnificent*

Another large species, the male magnificent looks dark and mysterious until the light catches his brilliant purple cap and green throat. Females are duller gray and green. This species spends the summer in Southwest mountain forests.

## THE WESTERN COUSIN
### *Black-chinned*

West of the Great Plains, this bird is often seen in yards, parks and along riversides each summer. It's a close relative of the ruby-throat, and it looks nearly identical, except the male's throat is black and bright purple, not red. Even its voice, with soft whistles and chatters, sounds the same.

Black-chinned

## THE BACKYARD SUPERSTAR
### *Ruby-throated*

This backyard favorite is the only nesting species in the eastern half of the United States and Canada. Most migrate to the tropics in winter, but a few remain in the southeastern states. The male has a green back, whitish belly and brilliant ruby red on the lower throat.

Calliope

Ruby-throated

## THE TINY MARVEL
### *Calliope*

North America's smallest bird, the calliope is barely longer than 2 inches. The male is known by his striped throat, with rays of red-violet and white. Females are tiny and plain. Spending the summer in the Northwest, calliopes go to Mexico for the winter.

## THE WINTER CHAMPION
### *Anna's*

All along the Pacific Coast and east into Arizona, Anna's stick around all year, even through the winter. The male has a brilliant rosy red color on his throat and the top of his head. He draws attention to himself by perching up high and singing a scratchy, buzzy song.

## HOT SPOTS

Visit one of these hummingbird hot spots and cross more species off your life list.

- Ramsey Canyon Preserve, Arizona
- Davis Mountains State Park, Texas
- Rio Grande Valley, Texas
- Cabrillo National Monument, California
- Bandelier National Monument, New Mexico

## THE FIREBALL
### *Rufous*

Shining bright coppery orange like a new penny and with a fiery throat to match, the male rufous zooms around western habitats in summer, as far north as southeastern Alaska. Tiny but spunky, he often chases other hummingbirds away from feeders and flowers. Most of these birds go to Mexico in winter, but some stay and spend the season in Southeast gardens.

Allen's

## THE LOOKALIKE
### *Allen's*

Nearly identical to the rufous, Allen's live mainly along the California coast, although they spread eastward during migration. Adult males have a bright green center back, instead of coppery brown. Females and young ones are almost impossible to identify.

**See Anna's, broad-billed and violet-crowned hummingbirds at the Paton Center for Hummingbirds just outside of Patagonia, Arizona.**

## THE ARIZONA GEM
### *Broad-billed*

Shining dark green and blue, with a bright red bill, the male broad-billed is hard to miss in a few parts of southern Arizona but is hardly ever seen elsewhere. The female has a plain gray belly.

## THE FLASHY GIANT
### *Blue-throated*

Almost the size of a sparrow, the blue-throated is the largest breeding hummingbird in the U.S. It lives along shady canyons in mountains near the Mexican border. The blue on its throat is hard to see, but its spectacular tail pattern is obvious: blue-black with big white patches.

## WALLFLOWERS IN FOCUS
*Female hummingbirds deserve attention, too!* Adult male hummingbirds are colorful showoffs and typically easy to identify. But the females and juveniles of most North American species look the same: greenish on the back and whitish or grayish on the underparts, with small white spots on the tail feathers. It takes an expert to identify subtle differences in shape, color and call notes. So don't fret if a female or juvenile has you stumped.

## THE WING-SINGER
### *Broad-tailed*

In western mountain meadows, you know the male broad-tailed is coming because his wings make a musical, metallic trilling sound when he flies. He's emerald green on the back and sides, and rosy red on the throat. Females are plainer, mostly green and white with orange sides.

## THE DESERT DWELLER
### *Costa's*

In Southern California and Arizona, this tough little bird manages to find flowers even in the desert. The male wears a purple cap and a purple throat patch that flares out to the sides. In early spring, he sings a thin, whistled song, sometimes while zooming through the air in a courtship-display dive.

Costa's

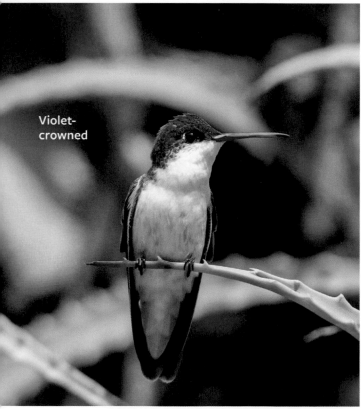

Violet-crowned

Lucifer

## THE SPLASH OF WHITE
### *Violet-crowned*

Many hummingbirds have whitish bellies, but the violet-crowned is the only one that's bright snowy white from chin to undertail. The red bill and purple cap are bonus marks. Violet-crowneds are seen mainly in summer along rivers in southern Arizona and southwestern New Mexico.

## THE BORDER BANDIT
### *Lucifer*

A curved bill and flaring purple throat patch mark the male Lucifer. Females have buff or pale rust-colored throats. These birds are distinctive summer residents of dry canyons near the border from western Texas to southern Arizona.

## WIRE-CRESTED THORNTAIL

When you see a male wire-crested thorntail, you immediately notice the incredible wispy green crest, the bold white stripe across the lower back, and his long, forked tail. It's difficult to get a good look at this bird because it typically hovers and feeds on flowers high in the tree canopy.

# 1,600

**MORE THAN** 1,600 bird species are found in Ecuador—twice as many as in the U.S.

## RAINBOW STARFRONTLET

The name itself makes this one of the most special hummingbirds, and the plumage does not disappoint. As if its coppery-colored body and glowing green throat weren't enough, this species sports all the colors of the rainbow on its crown.

## LONG-TAILED SYLPH

The most distinctive thing about this species is its extremely long tail. The shimmering blue-green color extends up to the crown, making the bird look, in the right light, as if it is glowing. Because this species has a short bill, it sometimes pierces the base of flowers to drink nectar.

## 17

**RICH IN BIODIVERSITY,** Ecuador is one of only 17 countries classified as megadiverse.

## SPANGLED COQUETTE

Although tiny, this one is truly spectacular. The incredible orange crest, glistening green throat and rufous tail create a striking color combination. Spotting this bird is a real treat because it's a rare and difficult species to find.

## GIANT

There is no better name for the largest hummingbird species in the world. With its slower and deeper wing beats than others, this cinnamon-colored bird may remind you more of a swift or a swallow than a typical hummingbird as it zips by.

# Grow a Buffet for Birds

*Hummingbirds flock to blooms in every color of the rainbow.*  BY DEB WILEY

**1**

**BLOOM TIME**
Variety is essential for attracting ruby-throats and other hummingbirds. Plant this cardinal flower for consecutive blooms.

### 1 Cardinal flower

*LOBELIA CARDINALIS*
ZONES 2 TO 9
SIZE: 3 TO 4 FEET TALL,
1 TO 2 FEET WIDE

Cardinal flower, named for the red robes worn by Roman Catholic cardinals, needs mulch to retain moisture during summer and protect its root system during cold northern winters.

**Why we love it:** This deer-resistant, reseeding and self-rooting perennial lights up partial shade or full sun areas that boast consistently moist soil. Flower spikes open from bottom to top and stay in bloom for weeks.

### 2 Bee balm

*MONARDA SPECIES*
ZONES 4 TO 9
SIZE: 1 TO 4 FEET TALL
AND WIDE

For a surefire way to attract hummingbirds, grow bee balm. Whether you choose native or cultivated varieties, the birds can't resist the nectar-rich blooms. Bee balm needs sun, moist soil and plenty of air circulation to ward off powdery mildew.

**Why we love it:** After the tubular pink, red, white or violet flowers fade, the round seed heads add beauty in fall and winter and may self-sow.

### 3 Penstemon

*PENSTEMON SPECIES*, ZONES 3 TO 9; SIZE: 1 TO 4 FEET TALL

Penstemons are North American natives that come in many forms. It's best to plant those that are native to your area. They're low-maintenance if you place them in full sun and soil with excellent drainage; they hate wet feet, especially in the winter.

**Why we love it:** The options are nearly limitless. Choose from a wide palette of flower colors, including white, yellow, blue, purple, red and orange.

---

**THE BEST KIND OF BLOOMS** *Hummingbird-friendly flowers have three things in common. Their flowers are tube-shaped and brightly colored, they're scentless, and they grow where it's easy for hummingbirds to hover and sip.*

---

### 4 Hosta

*HOSTA SPECIES*, ZONES 3 TO 9
SIZE: 6 TO 30 INCHES

Although most hostas are grown for their leaves, the large bell-shaped blooms are excellent nectar sources in hues of purple to white.

**Why we love it:** Everyone thinks of hummingbird plants for sunny areas, but the little fliers like a sweet treat in the shade, too.

### 5 Catmint
NEPETA SPECIES, ZONES 3 TO 9
SIZE: 1 TO 3 FEET TALL, OFTEN
WIDER THAN IT IS TALL

Catmints are easy to grow, long-blooming, heat-tolerant, and deer- and pest-resistant. After the flowers fade, shear off the spent blooms and about a third of the stalk for a second round.
**Why we love it:** Hummingbirds feed from all kinds of catmint but especially love Siberian catmint's blue blooms (*Nepeta sibirica*). Just be aware that this variety can be an aggressive grower.

### 6 Agastache
AGASTACHE SPECIES, ZONES 4
TO 9; SIZE: 1 TO 5 FEET TALL

It's no coincidence that a common name for one of the agastache species is hummingbird mint. That type excels in dry regions. Choose anise hyssop (*Agastache foeniculum*) in northern, wetter climates. Tiny tubular flowers on slender stalks grow in a variety of colors and shapes. Full sun and excellent drainage are essential for keeping plants happy.
**Why we love it:** Deer and rabbits leave it alone.

### 7 Eastern red columbine
AQUILEGIA CANADENSIS, ZONES 3 TO 8
SIZE: 1 TO 3 FEET TALL, 1 FOOT WIDE

This easy-to-grow perennial performs in part to full shade. It reseeds itself to replenish older plants, which tend to lose vigor after three or four years. The airy habit allows it to grow among other plants.
**Why we love it:** Sure, you can find cultivated varieties of columbines, but native columbine, with its crimson spurs and bright yellow stamens, is an early-season favorite.

---

**SEEING RED** *Hummingbirds love red for a very good reason. Their eyes are tuned to the rosy hue because their retinas have a dense concentration of cones, which mute cooler shades like blue and heighten warmer shades like red and yellow.*

---

Honeysuckle is perfectly shaped for hummingbirds, like this ruby-throat.

### 8 Honeysuckle
LONICERA SEMPERVIRENS, ZONES 4 TO 10
SIZE: 10- TO 20-FOOT VINE

If you have a fence, arbor or trellis in full sun to part shade, plant a colorful trumpet honeysuckle vine and watch the hummingbirds go absolutely wild for this climber.
**Why we love it:** After a flush of blooms in late spring, flowers continue sporadically until fall. Prune or don't prune—your choice.

**9**

## 9 Salvia

*SALVIA* SPECIES, ANNUAL TO
PERENNIAL ZONES 3 TO 10
SIZE: 1 TO 6 FEET TALL

Pick a salvia, any type of salvia—just as hummingbirds do. The tubular flowers are just right for dipping a beak into. Salvias grow best in full sun to part shade. **Why we love it:** Almost continuously blooming, especially in hot, dry conditions, salvias come in a huge selection of colors and plant habits.

Ruby-throated
hummingbird

**KEEP THEM HAPPY**
*Here's what keeps the hummingbirds coming back each year.*
- Insects and spiders that are often attracted to the same flowers.
- Water. Nectar is sticky, so hummingbirds like to bathe in either shallow moving water or spray mist.
- Nesting material, such as mosses and other fine-textured plants.
- A pesticide-free yard.

## 10 Zinnia

*ZINNIA* ELEGANS, ANNUAL
SIZE: 6 TO 48 INCHES TALL

Zinnias are a treat for hummingbirds and humans. The birds sip from the central florets, and you can snip the blooms to create indoor bouquets. **Why we love it:** There are so many colors to choose from! If you're planting a rainbow of flower colors and need green, choose Queen Lime, Envy, Tequila Lime or chartreuse varieties.

**10**

# Flashes of Red

*Quick! Prep your feeders and fill your garden with tubular flowers for a chance to see ruby-throated hummingbirds, one of the most popular fliers in the east.*

**SHINY & BRIGHT**
When the sun hits it just right, a male ruby-throated hummingbird's gorget, or throat, is a beautiful iridescent red. His vibrant green head glows, too!

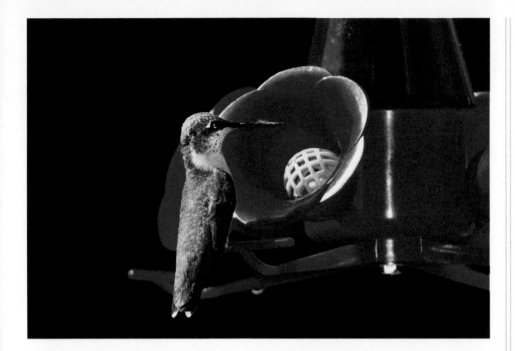

**WHEN TO STOP FEEDING**
As ruby-throated hummingbirds move south in late summer and early fall, they need food sources to fuel their migration. To make sure you feed any stragglers, a good rule of thumb is to leave your feeders up for a week or two after you see the last hummingbird pass by.

**RUFOUS SIGHTINGS**
Although uncommon, a rufous hummingbird occasionally finds its way into the southeastern United States.

**MAGNIFICENT MIGRANTS**
Some ruby-throats fly more than 3,000 miles from Canada to Costa Rica. That's quite a feat for a bird that weighs a little less than 4 grams.

Several hummingbird species are sprinkled over the western half of North America, but only one, the ruby-throat, flies the eastern skies regularly. As the region's tiniest birds, ruby-throated hummingbirds generate a lot of buzz and excitement when they choose your backyard.

Males steal the show with green bodies and ruby red throats that glisten like jewels in the sunlight. Females aren't as grandiose in appearance. They sport green backs, white underparts and black masks near their eyes. All juveniles look so similar to females that it's often nearly impossible to tell which it is. Whether a male, female or youngster chooses your yard, their acrobatic, territorial and erratic antics always entertain.

Ruby-throats zip, zoom and dart through gardens, woodland edges and parks from one food source to another. Because they constantly burn energy while on the move, they may eat up to three times their body weight in a day. To find that much nectar, one bird might visit hundreds of flowers per day, which is why a hummingbird-friendly backyard is so important.

Attracting ruby-throats is easy when you cater to their sweet tooth with feeders and flowers. A sugar-water feeder is the quickest way to jump-start your hummingbird haven. Buy a basic red plastic feeder from any big-box store or online. Choose one with a built-in ant moat and yellow bee guards to keep the pests away and your fast-flying guests safe.

Fill your feeders with a mixture of four parts water to one part table sugar. Boil and let it cool. Although hummingbirds love red, it's not necessary (and may even be harmful) to dye your mix red with food coloring. Clear sugar water gets the job done just as well.

Nectar-rich tubular flowers are another way for backyard birders in the east to lure ruby-throats. Bee balm, salvia, coral honeysuckle and fuchsia are popular with hummers, offering the vibrant colors they love and easy access to nectar.

However, the sweet stuff covers just one dietary need. Ruby-throated hummingbirds also require protein to survive, and they get their fill of it from small insects, such as mosquitoes, gnats and fruit flies. They eat spiders, too.

In the summer, food sources such as sugar water, flowers and bugs are especially important as young ruby-throats seek nutrition and prepare for fall migration.

Males tend to start the trek first, sometimes heading south as early as July. Watch for flashes of ruby as these eastern favorites take off.

Broad-tailed
hummingbird

**BALCONY
BENEFITS**
Whether you lure
hummingbirds
to a small patio
or a high-rise
balcony, you get
to watch them
feed from
the comfort
of your home.

# High-Rise Hummingbirds

*Tempt birds to your balcony with flashy flowers and a trio of tricks.* **BY SALLY ROTH**

Hummingbirds fly forward, backward, sideways...and up, up, up! They go where the food is, and to the colors they love most: red, orange and even rich pink. If you think about it, flowering trees, such as redbud, eucalyptus and mimosa, are nectar favorites, and they're way above the ground. Hummingbirds have even been spotted checking out rooftop gardens of towering buildings in large cities, so the sky really is the limit.

To make your high-level offerings truly stand out, focus on vivid flowers. For a sunny balcony, geraniums are a solid choice. Their bloom clusters are huge and draw the eye of humans and hummingbirds alike from a distance. But geraniums are generally scanty in nectar, so add a pot or rail box of nectar-rich nasturtiums (long-blooming and easy to start from seed), New Guinea impatiens or other hummingbird-friendly flowers to keep the nectar-seekers there once they arrive. If your balcony is on the shady side, annual shade impatiens (*Impatiens walleriana*) offer a satisfying nectar source and a highly visible attraction.

Maybe your thumb isn't the greenest. Have no fear—you can always fake it! Wrap a length of red-flowered garland around the rail, stick sprays of fake geraniums into a vase on a bistro table, or fill a railing window box with the brightest red and orange artificial flowers you can find.

Fake blooms work fine to attract their attention, but the birds won't stick around once they discover your trick. So make sure there's a sweet payoff. If you use artificial flowers to attract hungry birds, add mini nectar feeders on wire stems to your flowerpots, and make sure your full-size feeder is full of sugar water, close by and visible.

One last trick to get the most out of your high-rise hummingbird haven: Add perches. The tiny birds spend as much as 80 percent of their waking hours at rest. They prefer a relatively high perch with a clear view, so straighten out a wire coat hanger (the perfect diameter for those tiny feet), twist one end onto the railing and bend the top horizontally to provide a lookout. When the busy little birds have an inviting place to sit and rest between rounds of feeding, even high-rise hummingbirds linger a little longer.

> "Can any other bird rival it in agility? Or vie with it in its simple grace?"
>
> VALSA GEORGE

**SMALL YET MIGHTY**
Hummingbirds may not look it, but they are tiny powerhouses. Most North American species beat their wings between 50 and 100 times per second, and Anna's reach flying speeds of 60 miles per hour during courtship displays.

**LURE MORE** hummingbirds with moving water. Add a solar fountain to a bath or a small dish with this kit from *thebirdhousechick.com*

# hello, hummingbirds!

*The key to the tiny flier's heart is through its stomach. Make your backyard a sugar-water hot spot with these top tips.*

**BY RACHAEL LISKA**

Ruby-throats jockey for a prime spot at a sugar-water feeder.

*i*t's a magical moment when a hummingbird comes to call. These flying dynamos, arguably the crown jewels of backyard birds, are among nature's most beautiful and fascinating creatures. Once you know what they're looking for, hosting them in your backyard is easy. Now let's lay out the welcome mat!

This rufous plunges his straight, slender bill into a feeder for sugar water.

**GO RED.** With one of the fastest metabolisms in the animal kingdom, hummingbirds are always on the lookout for nectar to fuel their busy bodies. As it turns out, hummingbirds have a heightened visual sensitivity to red flowers, so they tend to visit blooms in these hues. Perennials like cardinal flower, bee balm and garden phlox and annuals like snapdragon, flowering tobacco and pentas are excellent varieties to plant. Another option is to set out a bright red sugar-water feeder—or tie a large red bow to one.

Bold red blooms, like this azalea, are magnets for hummingbirds.

A bee guard keeps bees out but allows this rufous's beak in.

*bee guard*

## GET THE RIGHT MIX.

Hummingbirds love sugar water. Bird expert, author and longtime *Birds & Blooms* contributor George Harrison recommends making the perfect batch by mixing 1 part sugar (no artificial sweeteners, please) with 4 parts water. Bring to a boil, cool completely and then fill your feeder. Leftovers may be refrigerated for up to a week, so consider making extra. Trust us: The hummingbirds can't get enough once they get a taste of the sweet stuff.

## KEEP A TIDY FEEDER.

Ensure that contents stay fresh by filling feeders halfway and changing the mixture every three to five days. Keeping it out of the hot sun also helps. If a feeder does develop mold inside, clean it with hot water and vinegar or a mild detergent. For tough spots, use a bottle brush, or fill the feeder with sand and water and shake vigorously.

## BANISH BEES.

Avoid unwanted guests by choosing a feeder designed to discourage these pests. "Feeder ports should be large enough for a hummingbird's beak but small enough that a bee can't crawl through them," says H. Ross Hawkins, founder and executive director of The Hummingbird Society. "Ideally, the nectar should sit far enough below the port opening, ¼ to ½ inch, so that bees can't access it. While many feeders don't address this problem, basin-style ones are usually excellent in this department."

## TRICK THE BULLIES.

Sure, they look sweet, but these birds can get downright territorial when food is on the line! To prevent one hummingbird from alienating swarms of others, set two or three of the feeders out of sight from one another. Problem solved!

## PUT OUT PROTEIN.

Besides the carbohydrates that nectar provides, hummingbirds crave protein from insects. "Put a few chunks of banana, melon or other overripe fruit into a mesh bag, such as an old onion bag," suggests author and bird expert Laura Erickson. "Fruit flies may gather, and you can watch your hummingbirds dart about to catch them in midair. Plus, cleanup is a snap since you can throw the bag away when done."

Calliope hummingbird

**These ruby-throats** come back to my front yard every year, and I love to sit and watch them. Occasionally, things really get out of hand when 15 or so try to feed at the same time.
**Clatis Tew** BUTLER, ALABAMA

**Ever vigilant,** this female rufous guarded the feeder in my yard, attacking other rufous and black-chinned hummingbirds with unbridled alacrity, then returning to this perch as lookout. What makes this photo special is her protruding tongue, which shows a flash of the beautiful bird's personality.
**Allen Livingston** HUNTINGTON, UTAH

**TIP OF THE TONGUE**
Hummingbirds have split tongues that work like pumps to let them efficiently suck nectar.

Ruby-throated hummingbird
**PHOTO BY GILBERTO SANCHEZ**

Male rufous hummingbird
**PHOTO BY KOJI KANEMOTO**

Ruby-throated hummingbird
**PHOTO BY RICK HOPSON**

Female or young rufous hummingbird
**PHOTO BY TRACY JOHNSON**

# CHAPTER 3

# Bird & Bloom Essentials

Learn the basics for transforming your yard into a safe haven for your favorite winged visitors. Treat feathered friends using expert tips for food, birdbaths, pest control and more. Discover some creative ideas for containers and clever ways to save water.

**HOME TWEET HOME** American robins typically construct their nests in trees and shrubs below a layer of dense leaves, as in this red-flowered crabapple.

# Say Yes to the Nest

*Here's what to do when you come face-to-beak with a feathered family.*  BY RACHAEL LISKA

Birds gather twigs, twine and anything they can get their beaks on to create a cozy home for their families this time of year. With an increasing loss of natural habitat, it's only a matter of time until a budding brood moves into your backyard.

## A nest near your entryway

Where a bird chooses to build a nest is not always convenient for its human hosts. But remember, it isn't every day that you're given a front-row seat to one of the most exciting cycles of nature. If possible, be hospitable and find another way to enter your home. Your feathered visitors stay only for a handful of weeks. Alert anyone who might frequent the door, and keep pets away from the nesting area.

If there's no alternative way to enter, contact your local wildlife agency to ask for assistance. Moving a nest on your own may technically violate the law, and although some birds, like house sparrows and starlings, aren't protected by these laws, most bird species are covered.

## Abandoned nest with eggs

It's unlikely the adults have left their eggs. Many birds don't start incubating until the last egg is laid, which is why you might not see the parents for some time. Or maybe you've lingered too long and they're waiting for you to scram. Even spooked birds most likely will return within a day or two.

On the off chance that the pair does not return, it probably means the eggs are not viable. Give yourself plenty of time to come to this conclusion, however, and don't discard any nest or its contents without first reaching out to your local wildlife agency.

## A bird out of the nest

If the little one you've found has feathers, it's best not to interfere. That bird, called a fledgling, most likely left the confines of the nest on purpose. While it can't fly yet, a fledging spends a couple of days wandering around, hiding in shrubs or low branches. Rest assured its folks are waiting in the wings nearby. In fact, you may even hear their scolding calls if you get too close to their little one.

However, if you find a hatchling, which is a very young bird with no feathers, it probably fell out by accident. In this case, gently place the youngster back in the nest. If the nest is not accessible, set the nestling in a small container filled with shredded paper towel. Fasten it to the tree trunk or place it in a nearby shrub in hopes its parent will care for it. It's a common myth that birds abandon their babies upon human contact. But be sure to wash your hands after contact.

**CITIZEN SCIENCE**
Become a certified NestWatch monitor; visit active nests every three to four days and report your findings to the Cornell Lab of Ornithology. Get started at *nestwatch.org*

> **"** Thanks for this day, for all birds safe in their nests, for whatever this is, for life. **"**
> BARBARA KINGSOLVER

**PROTECTED BY LAW**
Most birds and their nests are protected by the Migratory Bird Treaty Act, which states that it is illegal to take, possess, import, export, transport, sell, purchase or barter any part of a nest or eggs unless you hold a valid permit.

**A robin with a mouthful of nesting material.**

**Squirrels steer clear of safflower.**

**NYJER**
Lure finches and chickadees with nyjer, a tiny black seed that is sometimes called thistle. Bonus! Bully birds tend to leave nyjer alone.

**SAFFLOWER**
Serve safflower in a hopper feeder for cardinals, grosbeaks and house finches to devour. Remember: It may take a while for the birds to get acquainted with the seed.

# Seeds Birds Love

*Maximize the traffic at your feeders with popular foods that keep birds coming back for more.* **BY BIRDS & BLOOMS EDITORS**

**The best all-around seed!**

**SUNFLOWER**
This food deserves the No. 1 spot in your yard! Sunflower seeds, both in the shell (*left*) and out-of-shell meats (*below, left*), appeal to finches, chickadees, nuthatches, grosbeaks, cardinals, jays and even some woodpeckers. Because sunflower seeds are delicious to so many species, including some large undesirable birds, they're best served in feeders that allow only small songbirds to perch on or to enter the feeding chamber.

### Choose the right feeder
**Tray feeders** are flat platforms that attract a variety of seed-eaters. Look for ones that have holes to allow rain or snow drainage.

**Tube feeders** are cylinders with mesh or plastic-coated wire screens. They're great for small birds, such as finches, chickadees and nuthatches.

**Hopper feeders** have an enclosed reservoir for seeds that slides food down to the open feeding tray below. Plus, seed stays dry! Woodpeckers, grosbeaks and blue jays frequent these feeders.

# Birdbath Basics

*For a robust bird population, just add fresh water!*
*Lure more species to your backyard with these six tips.*

**BY KIRSTEN SWEET**

**1.** Shallow basins are best. The water should be no deeper than 2 inches in the middle and ½ to 1 inch at the edges.

**2.** Place rocks or stones in the middle of your bath for birds to perch and drink without getting their feet wet.

**3.** Nestle baths in a shady spot (to keep water fresh) that is near trees or shrubs, but not so near that predators can lurk in ambush. When a bird is taking a dip and a predator flies by, it needs a safe place.

**4.** Add motion with a dripper, fountain or mister. The noise and movement catches a bird's attention better than standing water. Bonus! Hummingbirds love a light mist!

**5.** Clean and rinse your bath every couple of days and then add fresh water. Grab a wire brush for a really deep clean if algae forms.

**6.** Pedestal baths allow you to watch birds splish-splashing around right from your window. Consider a ground-level bath, too. It mimics natural water sources and lures birds that like to stay low.

> Water is the ticket to attracting a variety of species, even those that shy away from feeders.

### BIRDBATH IN A SNAP!

Your feathered friends won't mind if you recycle. Give a trash can lid, old pan or flowerpot tray new life as a quick and easy birdbath.

**Purchase birdbaths at your local big-box store, garden center, specialty bird store or online.**

### HORIZONTAL BAR
Multiple ports on a bar feeder can mean many hummingbirds at once, which is always a treat. But cross your fingers that these territorial birds make friends instead of foes. Prevent any power trips by setting up several feeders.

### SAUCER
Flying saucer-shaped feeders are backyard favorites for a reason. They're super easy to clean and refill, and the sugar water is usually far enough below the feeding ports that pesky bugs can't dive in for a sweet snack. A built-in ant moat provides additional protection.

# Choose the Right Feeder
*There's no limit when it comes to serving up sugar water, so pick the perfect option for your backyard hummingbirds.*

### CLASSIC PLASTIC
Hummingbird newbies can't go wrong when you use a standard sugar-water feeder. There's nothing fancy about this backyard staple, but the plastic is easy to clean and the bright red color is extra-attractive to hummingbirds. Plus, many of these classics come with a built-in ant moat, which prevents hungry pests from crawling inside to sample the sweet stuff.

Add a pop of style with a glass feeder.

### ARTSY GLASS
If you already have a robust and hungry hummingbird population in your yard, try a feeder with a bit more flair. Chic and stylish glass feeders, like this one, may be a challenge to clean, and there's no perch for the birds to linger. However, it's a fun way to see how hummingbirds hover.

# Pests Be Gone!

*Discover seven natural ways to keep backyard bugs away from feeders.* BY SHERYL DEVORE

Feeders filled with sugar water or jelly attract sweet-tooth birds, such as hummingbirds and orioles. But sometimes, not-so-welcome guests, including ants, wasps and bees, crawl into feeders and create problems. "You can deter insects while remembering they're part of nature, too," says Emma Greig, the project leader for Project FeederWatch of the Cornell Lab of Ornithology.

For frustrated backyard birders, it may be tempting to use pesticides or oils to deter bugs, but Emma advises against these options because they may harm birds as well as the bees whose populations are declining. Instead, try some of these all-natural solutions to keep pests away. The birds (and bees!) will thank you.

- **Choose red saucer feeders.** With their super long tongues, hummingbirds can reach the nectar—but insects can't. Plus, while hummingbirds prefer the color red, bees are attracted to yellow.

Bee guards keep these calliope hummingbirds happy at the feeders.

- **Attach an ant moat,** typically about 3 inches wide and 1 to 2 inches deep, above jelly and sugar-water feeders. Because ants can't swim, water is an effective deterrent. Make moats or buy feeders with moats built in. Keep the feeder clean and filled with water.
- **Hang feeders with fishing line,** which is too thin for ants to climb.
- **Slip nectar guard tips** over the hummingbird feeder holes. These nectar guards block insects like yellow jackets, but hummingbirds can still get to the nectar. You can buy them or create your own mesh guard out of an onion bag.
- **Periodically move the feeders** by 3 or 4 feet. Birds will still find them easily, but insects often won't.
- **Hang a few fake wasps' nests** in protected areas to deter real wasps, which are territorial and typically won't venture into a place they think is already occupied.
- **Plant bee- and hummingbird-friendly food sources** in hanging baskets and around your garden. Try annuals like fuchsia and impatiens and perennials like trumpet vine, bee balm and milkweed.

**CHECK FOR LEAKS** Summer's heat may cause nectar in a feeder to expand and leak out. Keep pests at bay with a clean, leak-free feeder.

Male calliope hummingbird

# Take a Closer Look

*Discover how binoculars quickly bring your favorite birds into focus.* BY KIRSTEN SWEET

**DIOPTER RING**
Move the ring to adjust this side's ocular lens. It allows for differences in your eyes and focuses your view correctly.

**EYECUP**
Here's a tip! If you wear glasses, the eyecups should be twisted down. Sans spectacles? Twist up.

**OCULAR LENS**
These lenses, closest to your eyes, magnify the object.

**HINGE**
It connects the two barrels. Hold the eyecups to your eyes and pivot the barrels until you see one circle-shaped image.

**FOCUS WHEEL**
Adjust the wheel to move the ocular lenses simultaneously and bring the object into focus.

**OBJECTIVE LENS**
These large lenses gather light. The bigger the lens, the more light it captures, which means a brighter scene.

**BINS:** birder jargon for binoculars

**BARRELS**
The magic happens here! Each barrel works like a mini telescope to deliver a clear, crisp image.

## BEFORE YOU BUY

**1.** Go to a store and try out different brands and types of binoculars. Make sure the ones you pick are not heavy on your neck or too bulky for your hands.

**2.** Many birdwatchers use an 8x42 model, a good all-around size. That means an object appears eight times closer and the objective lens diameter is 42 millimeters.

**3.** The more you pay, the better and more durable the bins, but you don't have to break the bank. Start with a waterproof model and work up from there.

# Spot This Species

*Listen for the* potato-chip *call, and use these hints to ID American goldfinches when they stop for sunflowers.* BY KIRSTEN SWEET

*Solid black forehead*

*Yellow feathers on back, breast and belly*

*Black wings with white wing marks*

*Pinkish cone-shaped bill to crack open seeds (goldfinches love sunflower and thistle!)*

*Size: much smaller than a robin (one bird weighs about half an ounce)*

*Foot with three toes in front and one in back for perching on small branches and stems*

**WARDROBE CHANGE**
Male American goldfinches lose their drab winter feathers and bright yellow ones appear (shown here). In fall, their vibrancy fades as plain brown feathers grow in, and they transform to look more like females. The full molting process may take six to eight weeks, and during that time goldfinches appear patchy.

# Container Combos

*With blooming beauties like petunias, salvias and calibrachoas, your backyard becomes a popular hummingbird hot spot in no time. Get growing in a snap with these easy planting plans from Proven Winners.* **BY KIRSTEN SWEET**

Whether you have a sprawling landscape or a small patio, growing nectar-rich blooms in pots is a no-fail way to boost the hummingbird and butterfly population in your garden. These cherished fliers flock to colorful flowers that are nestled into favorite pots. The major benefit of this small-space strategy is placing the pots wherever you need to—near a sugar-water feeder, a shady corner or a sunny balcony. Try these two combos, or mix and match with other hummingbird favorites!

A

B       B

C

12-inch pot

**A**
**ABLAZIN' PURPLE SALVIA**
*Quantity: 1*

**B**
**COLORBLAZE LIME TIME**
**COLEUS** *Quantity: 2*

**C**
**SUPERBELLS EVENING STAR**
**CALIBRACHOA** *Quantity: 1*

## THE DIRT ON DIRT

It's tempting to toss some dirt from the garden right into your containers, but a potting mix that includes vermiculite, peat moss, compost, perilite or a combination of these materials yields the best results.

A    B

B    A

16-inch pot

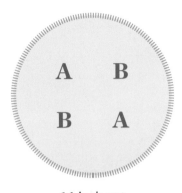

### A
**SURFINIA SKY
BLUE PETUNIA** *Quantity: 2*

### B
**SUPERTUNIA MINI ROSE
VEINED PETUNIA** *Quantity: 2*

## STONE

**Pros:** Strong and sturdy in all weather, a stone container insulates well against extreme temps.

**Cons:** Due to the heavy weight, stone pots are difficult to move around. Color options are also limited, and proper drainage can be tricky.

## TERRA-COTTA

**Pros:** An all-time classic, terra-cotta looks good holding almost any kind of plant, and its porous surface means a decreased chance of root rot. Plus, style options are limitless with the addition of a fresh coat of paint.

**Cons:** It absorbs moisture, which means pots are susceptible to cracking in freezing weather, and plants need to be watered more often.

# Find the Perfect Pot

*With endless options on the market, choose the right home for every potted plant on your porch.*

## PLASTIC

**Pros:** Easy on the wallet, plastic pots come in all shapes, sizes and colors. Soil retains moisture, so gardeners can water their plants less frequently. There are also self-watering varieties for an even more hands-off approach.

**Cons:** This material may fade in the sun, and a strong wind can blow one of these lightweights over if it's not properly weighted down.

## RESIN & FIBERGLASS

**Pros:** Colors won't fade as fast compared to plastic, and there's a multitude of choices when it comes to design and size, so these containers mesh with any gardener's style and space.

**Cons:** Single-walled containers crack easily in subzero temps, and if they undergo power-washing, they may be susceptible to fraying. Resin and fiberglass options may also be more expensive than their plastic counterparts.

# 7 Ways to Be Water-Wise

*Quench your garden's thirst and save time and money on watering, too.*

**RISE AND SHINE!** Water your plants, like the sedge, Autumn Joy sedum and artemisia shown here, first thing in the morning, when temps are cool and evaporation rates are low.

It's possible to reduce outdoor water use by 20 to 50 percent with a few easy changes. To keep your water bill low and plants in their prime, try these tips from the National Garden Bureau and the Gardener's Supply Co.

**1** Use organic matter, such as compost, chopped-up leaves or composted manure, to supplement your soil. These organic materials increase the water-holding capacity of soil. A good rule of thumb is to add 1 inch of compost per year.

**2** Give your plants a solid soak. While sprinklers get the job done, a soaker hose is even better. It applies the water directly to the soil by the roots, so up to 90 percent is actually available to plants.

**3** Spread mulch. It prevents weeds from growing and soaking up all of the water you add to the planting area. A layer of mulch provides the most bang for your buck. Organic types are best; try grass clippings free of weedkillers, evergreen needles and shredded leaves.

**4** Be extra frugal and capture all of the free water you can by placing rain barrels or a cistern at your downspouts. A 1,000-square-foot roof collects about 625 gallons of water from just 1 inch of rain.

**5** Know the characteristics of your planting site, such as the amount of sun and shade it receives, soil type and wind conditions. Make a plan to group plants with similar needs.

**6** Shop with drought-tolerance in mind. Some plants get all the water they need from rain, so once established, they require less attention. If you're looking for perennials suited for drought conditions, your best bet is usually native plants that are adapted to your climate and soil type.

**7** Keep up with garden chores. Healthy plants mean less work! When you stay on top of tasks such as weeding, thinning and pruning, you add to the health of your plants and, in turn, need to water less frequently.

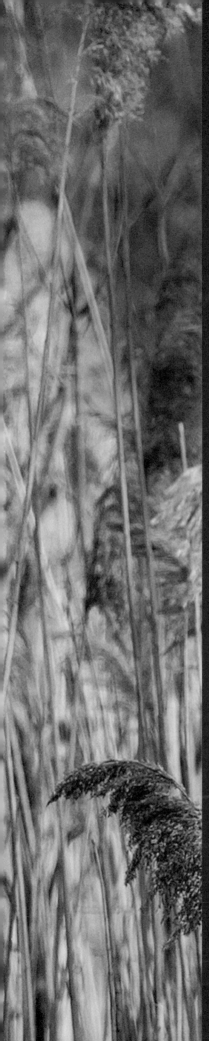

JOHANN SCHUMACHER DESIGN

# CHAPTER 4

# Attracting Birds

There's nothing quite as rewarding as creating a sanctuary in your backyard for flying friends. From cardinals and owls to juncos and goldfinches, birds of a feather will flock to your space if you follow the simple ideas and suggestions offered in this info-packed section.

# create a
# *BIRD-SAFE*
# backyard

*Keep your favorite feathered friends
healthy with clean feeders, fresh
birdseed and a natural yard.*

**BY KENN AND
KIMBERLY KAUFMAN**

Bring on the
eastern bluebirds
with a garden free
of pesticides.

# A *lot of* planning, time and money

go into attracting and feeding your backyard birds. But making your space appealing to them with food and plants they love is only one part of the equation. You also need to ensure that birds stay safe while in your yard. With these tips, you are on your way to a bustling backyard full of feathered guests.

**Look at the windows of your house from a bird's perspective.**

### PREVENT PAINFUL PANES

When you hear a bird crash into a window, a feeling of dread comes over you. Stand in your backyard and look at the windows of your house from a bird's perspective, and it's easy to see why strikes are a major issue. Windows reflect the sky and fool birds into thinking they can fly through them.

Special tape, decals shaped like hawks and many other products designed to reduce window strikes are effective and worth trying. If you're experiencing bird strikes at windows near your feeders and decals aren't doing the trick, move the feeders to within 2 or 3 feet of the window. In such a short distance, birds can't build up any speed between the feeder and the window. Birds may still bump into the window occasionally, but they're far less likely to be injured.

Change out birdbath water every other day to keep song sparrows coming back for more.

**GROW NATURAL!**
A pesticide-free yard is the safest option for your favorite birds, other wildlife guests, pets and you, too!

## SAY NO TO PESTICIDES

Birding and gardening go hand-in-hand, and understanding how birds, bugs and plants benefit one another greatly enhances the rewards. As an active gardener, you probably have found bugs eating your plants and felt the urge to take action. But it's important to know that most pesticides are nondiscriminate killers that don't just eliminate specific bugs. Pesticides kill important pollinators, like honeybees and butterflies, as well as helpful insects like lady beetles.

Although many kinds of lawn fertilizers with weed killers are harmful to wildlife, you still should consider organic fertilizers. Building your soil with a strong combination of compost and organic fertilizers is critical. If you forgo all fertilizers, you can end up with poor plant growth, fewer bugs for birds to eat, and soil erosion as plants decline.

And reducing the overall use of harsh pesticides in yards is healthier for humans, too.

**GARDEN WISELY** Compost and mulch reduce the need for pesticide use because they help healthy plants both outcompete the weeds and better tolerate pests.

Keep thistle feeders tidy to attract American and lesser goldfinches.

**CREATE AN OUTDOOR** enclosure or cat patio for your feline friend. They allow your kitty to be outdoors without being a threat to birds.

## CLEAN FEEDERS REGULARLY

Cleaning bird feeders is certainly not the most glamorous part of attracting birds, but it's necessary to keep them healthy and avoid spreading diseases. Moldy seeds and accumulated bird droppings create a very unhealthy environment. It's best to clean your feeders once a month using a stiff brush and hot, soapy water. Consider cleaning them more often during times of peak feeding activity, such as the migration season. Allow each feeder to dry completely before filling and putting it back up.

When you're ready to choose and buy a new feeder, it's important to consider how easy it will be for you to take apart and clean. Because many birds feed on the ground, remember to keep the area under the feeders clean as well.

Replace feeder nectar regularly to keep visiting ruby-throated hummingbirds healthy.

## KEEP CATS HAPPY INDOORS

Cats are lovely and make wonderful companions. But if you love birds and feeding them, it's best to keep your cats indoors. Studies prove the devastating impact that roaming house cats and feral cats have on birds and small mammals.

House cats are not native and also are not part of the natural ecosystem. Many people believe that a well-fed kitty wouldn't have any reason to hunt birds, but even cared-for cats have the instinct to go after birds. Feeders and roaming cats are a lethal combination. If you have an outdoor cat, or if many strays visit your yard, it may be best if you refrain from feeding the birds, for the birds' own safety. Remember that, according to veterinarians, indoor cats live longer, healthier lives. So keeping them inside not only protects the birds; it's also better for the cats.

Creating and maintaining a bird-safe yard requires a bit more work and dedication beyond simply putting up a feeder. But the peace of mind that comes with doing your part to keep birds safe is extremely rewarding.

### A CLEAR WAY TO FEED MORE HUMMINGBIRDS

**Beware:** Some retailers offer hummingbird food colored with red dye. Most leading experts agree that the dye can be harmful to birds, and at the very least it's unnecessary. The top recommendation for hummingbird food is to make it at home. Mix one part granulated white sugar to four parts water. Any other kind of sweetener besides white granulated table sugar may be unsafe.

# attract more CARDINALS

*For a backyard full of scarlet-hued fliers and their mates, grow plants they love to eat and shrubs to shelter their families.*

Dogwood trees and purple coneflowers (above right) provide food for cardinals.

S etting out a bird feeder filled with black oil sunflower seeds is a surefire way to attract northern cardinals—but ambitious gardeners shouldn't stop there, because the right plants bring in these ruby red beauties and other songbirds, too. The key is to focus on the trifecta of providing food, cover and places to raise young, says Gary Ritchison, an ornithologist at Eastern Kentucky University and writer of the bird guide *Northern Cardinal*. A deep dive into the life of cardinals unveils clues to help you attract the ubiquitous backyard birds.

## *clue#1*

### A BILL BUILT FOR SEED

The shape and structure of a cardinal's bill reveals the bird's food preference. The downward curve, typical of seed-eating birds, allows them to crack open or crush seeds. Cardinals also have larger jaw muscles than many other songbirds, which means they can consume bigger seeds. When you're selecting plants, look for those with medium-sized seeds as well as a mixture of seasonality.

Some seed-bearing plants to try: corn, Purple Majesty millet, nasturtium, purple coneflower, safflower, sunflower and sweet pea.

## *clue#2*

### YEAR-ROUND RESIDENTS

Although seeds are a favorite food, cardinals eat wild fruits, too. As nonmigratory birds, they seek a variety of foods as availability changes throughout the year.

But as they consume fruits, studies suggest, cardinals still are after the seeds, often discarding much of the fruit pulp. For that reason, fruits with larger seeds may be more attractive. Also look for a range of fruiting times and, since cardinals forage low to the ground, shorter varieties.

Berry plants to try: dogwood, hackberry, northern bayberry and serviceberry.

A northern cardinal nest is safely hidden away in the shelter of a boxwood shrub.

Dill attracts hungry butterfly and moth caterpillars that cardinal parents feed their nestlings.

## clue #3

### SCARLET FEATHERS

The vivid crimson color of male cardinals comes from carotenoid pigments, which are found in red fruits. Eating more of these scarlet-hued snacks, especially during molt, helps a male form brighter red feathers. The flashy color boosts his ability to successfully attract mates and defend a pair's nesting territory.

Red-fruited plants to try: hawthorn, raspberry, sumac and winterberry.

## clue #4

### INCOGNITO NESTS

For cardinal nests, concealment is key: The showy birds look for the camouflage of dense shrubs and trees. Compared to other birds, their nests are low, only 4 to 8 feet off the ground. Cardinals are territorial during breeding and the male stays near the nest, so to see cardinals year-round, host a nesting pair.

For their first nests in April or May, cardinals often choose the protection of evergreens. Pairs raise several broods a year and select different sites, so a mix of small, dense trees and shrubs is ideal. Wild grape is a good addition, too, because cardinals use its bark for nesting material.

Cover plants to try: box elder, eastern red cedar, hawthorn, nannyberry, rose and wild grape.

It's the male's turn to feed his ravenous brood of nestlings in their dogwood home.

# clue #5

## YOUNG MOUTHS TO FEED

Parent cardinals feed their young almost exclusively with insects, which provide the protein that nestlings need to grow muscle. When very young, the babies eat soft-bodied insects such as caterpillars. Planting additional beds of butterfly host plants is a good way to help stock the pantry for the weary parents.

For much of the year, 75 percent of the food that cardinals eat is plant material, but at the height of summer breeding season, the majority of their diet is insects.

Caterpillar host plants to try: dill, fennel, hollyhock, mustard greens and snapdragon.

# clue #6

## TREE DWELLERS

Often foraging on open ground, cardinals need to retreat quickly to safety. In summer, they use the same shrubs that provide nesting sites, but in winter, they escape to evergreens. During cold weather, cardinals form flocks that move around in search of food. So yards with plentiful food and cover have the best chance of hosting that picture-perfect vision of red dotting a snow-covered tree.

Evergreens to try: arborvitae, juniper and spruce.

## SUNFLOWER KINGS
*Tuck several of these sunny varieties around your yard.*

**Suntastic** is a dwarf multiflowered variety that blooms successive times and was a 2014 All-America Selections winner.

**Soraya** grows to about 6 feet with multiple sturdy branches, and it also was an AAS winner.

**Mammoth Grey Stripe, Mammoth Russian and Sunzilla** have enormous seed heads on towering stalks 12 to 16 feet tall.

**Aztec Gold, Royal Hybrid and Snack Sneed** are known for producing high-yield seeds the birds devour.

**FEEDING WITH FRIENDS**
Juncos are part of the sparrow family. Look for these dark-eyed beauties in flocks with other sparrows and bluebirds.

# Joy to the Juncos

*With the arrival of cool weather and fluffy white snow come flocks of pink-billed birds.*

BY KIRSTEN SWEET

Dark-eyed juncos reappear in many parts of the Lower 48 just as winter comes alive each year. They leave their breeding grounds in the North Woods and the western mountains to descend on backyard feeding stations across much of the U.S. Many people, like *Birds & Blooms* reader Jennifer Hardison from Athens, Tennessee, have a nickname for juncos. "We call them snowbirds because we only see them after a snowfall," she says.

To attract a whole flock of these backyard favorites to your own space, it takes a couple of feeders and the right plants to keep them full and coming back for more.

## Serve the Right Stuff

In winter, juncos feast on seeds of weeds and grasses that are left standing in your landscape or in fields, parks and open woodlands. Seeds from common plants such as chickweed, buckwheat, lamb's-quarters and sorrel make up 75 percent of their year-round diet. But juncos also supplement with feeder foods. These snowbirds prefer to forage on the ground for millet, sunflower hearts or cracked corn that has fallen from your feeders. They may occasionally steal a seed from a platform or tray feeder, or snatch a juicy berry from a fruit-producing shrub.

## East vs. West

Depending on where you live, your juncos may look different. Those found in the eastern half of the U.S. are charcoal gray on top with white bellies and known as slate-colored types. The most common variety in the west is called the Oregon junco. Male Oregons sport a solid black or slaty hood, chestnut-colored back, rusty sides and a white belly. Other juncos, like white-winged and gray-headed, are less common with limited ranges. Where junco ranges overlap, though, you may find several types in one winter flock. And when you do, look for their signature detail—a pretty pink bill.

**KEEP IT NATURAL**
Trees are key to luring red-bellieds to your yard. Alive or dead, trees provide plenty of places to forage or nest. Berry-producers like hawthorn and mountain ash are some favored food sources.

# Splash of Rosé

*Meet the woodpecker with a puzzling moniker and a big appetite for suet.* BY KEN KEFFER

Named for the hard-to-see, faint crimson color on their undersides, red-bellied woodpeckers are widespread in the eastern half of the United States. They're more common in the southern states, but the species is on the move, and the breeding range has extended north over the last century.

With zebralike stripes on their backs and wings, red-bellieds have a few look-alike relatives, such as the gila and golden-fronted woodpeckers of the Southwest. It's thanks to one distinguishable characteristic—a red head—that these woodpeckers are frequently confused with the less common red-headed woodpecker species, which shows a full head of bold red feathers.

And then there's the ambiguous red belly that makes many bird-watchers wonder if the person who named this woodpecker was seeing things. It's only when the light hits the stomach just right that the blush-colored feathers are most noticeable, and you finally see how this flier got its name.

Typical woodpecker features shared by red-bellieds include stiff tails to prop their bodies up against tree trunks, and feet with two toes facing forward and two pointing backward. It is this unique foot structure that helps the birds grasp branches and bark as they navigate up and around tree trunks on the hunt for insects.

Like so many species in the woodpecker family, male and female red-bellieds look slightly different. Males sport full red foreheads, caps and napes, while females have red napes and just a touch of ruby at the base of their bills. Their offspring, however, have plain, nondescript heads with a subdued red hue.

Both parents put in the work to incubate 4 to 6 eggs per clutch, with males often taking the night shift. It's not uncommon for the pair to aggressively defend their nest against potential predators, including starlings, snakes or even other woodpeckers.

To lure these lively and desirable woodpeckers to your backyard feeding station, serve a variety of their favorite foods. Suet is a must, especially in winter. Sunflower seeds and peanuts are a hit, too. And then, sweeten the deal with sugar water, fruit and jelly. As red-bellieds swoop in to your feeders for a snack, listen for the exuberant, guttural *quirr quirr quirr* chatter. Unlike most bird species, both males and females vocalize throughout the year. The sound is a favorite of many backyard birders.

"The bird's distinctive call announces its presence at our feeders," says *Birds & Blooms* reader Stephen Holland of Sandown, New Hampshire. "The unique coloring of a red head and striped back makes it stand out in all seasons."

**TOOLS FOR FORAGING**
Omnivorous red-bellied woodpeckers stick their barb-fringed tongues out 2 inches beyond their bills. This, and sticky saliva, helps them pluck insects from deep crevices.

**FOOD SAVERS**
In autumn, red-bellied woodpeckers store seeds and nuts in cracks in tree bark. They return to the spot for an easy-to-find meal come winter.

66 One of my favorites is the red-bellied woodpecker. They are so beautiful and very loyal to my feeders year-round. I just love watching them and enjoy their calls. 99
RA DEL HINCKLEY
BANCROFT, MICHIGAN

Faint red belly

# Be an Owl Landlord

*Roll out the welcome mat for these shadowy nighttime fliers.*

**BY KENN AND KIMBERLY KAUFMAN**

To lure eastern screech-owls, hang a nest box in February.

Owls are both popular and mysterious. They're so obscure, in fact, that most people report they've never seen one in real life. But some kinds of owls come into suburban neighborhoods and city parks, and they might even call your backyard home if you follow these four tips.

## Provide shelter.

Most kinds of owls like to hide inside dense cover during the day and venture out only at night. Evergreen trees provide this kind of shelter year-round. Depending on where you live, ideal choices include pine, spruce or juniper; check with a local native plant nursery to find out which grows best in your region. Eventually you may find long-eared owls, northern saw-whet owls, great horned owls or other species nestled away among the branches, sleeping the day away.

## Offer nest sites.

Eastern screech-owls are common and widespread east of the Rockies, with western screech-owls replacing them farther west, and both often lurk in towns and cities. However, to nest and raise young, they need cavities such as woodpecker holes or natural hollows in trees. If you can safely leave dead trees or large dead limbs standing, these often have holes that owls use. Otherwise, screech-owls use

Barn owls may raise their young inside man-made structures, like nest boxes, barns and even homes.

nest boxes designed for wood ducks or American kestrels, with an entrance hole at least 3 inches in diameter. In cooler climates, the northern saw-whet owl also adopts nest boxes, although it favors a 2-inch entrance hole.

Some larger owls also nest in cavities, including barn and barred owls. If you live in farm country, you may be able to place a barn owl box at the edge of open fields or in a barn loft. Barred owls favor dense, swampy woods, and they like boxes that are high in trees.

## PUT OUT NEST BOXES

Buy nest boxes designed for screech-owls or larger owls, or build your own. Check out *theraptortrust.org* for building plans, advice on placement and more.

### Say no to insecticides.

To successfully lure owls to your space, you have to also attract the creatures they hunt. Screech-owls feed on large insects, such as moths and beetles, and small animals such as mice. If you use insecticides or rodenticides around your garden, those poisons may wipe out the prey before the owls find them. Worse, the poisons may be passed along directly to the owls.

### Keep cats indoors.

Even if they're well-fed, prowling house cats kill many small wild animals. Wiping out populations of mice, voles, lizards and other creatures may not leave enough to support a family of screech-owls or other small owls. On the flip side, a cat that wanders outside at night might become a meal for a large species like a great horned owl. It's better for everyone to keep house cats inside of houses.

## Signs of Owls in Your Neighborhood

*They're masters of disguise, but look for these clues.*

### Sounds

Owls in towns and cities are often less vocal than those in wild country. But late at night, after traffic quiets down, listen for them calling.

### Pellets

Owls often swallow their food whole, later coughing up the indigestible parts. You may find "owl pellets" of matted fur, tiny bones, and insect scales under dense evergreens where the owls have roosted.

### Whitewash

When owls find a roosting spot, they may use it for several days. Their droppings accumulate as "whitewash" on the ground or on the tree trunk below their perch.

MARK TURNER

# CHAPTER 5

# Blooming Beauty

Your yard and garden will look their best when you learn great ways to care for them. It's time to say goodbye to landscape bare spots, sick plants and weeds. You'll also find suggestions for the brightest and best plants worth buying. Invite butterflies to stay for a bit with our helpful tips, too!

# Take Your Garden From
# GOOD TO GREAT

**13**

*Smart, easy tips to give your yard a boost.
From better potting mix to saying no to pesticides,
improve your yard with this gardener's dozen.*

Maximize space by planting in raised beds. Add supports and trellises for plants to grow up.

*No. 1*

### 1. Use the Best Enriched Potting Mix

Make looking after container plants much simpler by choosing a premium potting mix that's well-draining and has long-lasting nutrients. Look for potting soil with peat moss, pine bark and perlite or vermiculite. It's an easy-care way to achieve the best-ever displays.

### 2. Invest in Some Top-Notch Tools

Introduce a long-handled weeding fork to your gardening toolkit, and your knees and back will thank you. It's worth taking a look at what new tool designs are available. Many have been created with the goal of making garden tasks easier, reducing strain on joints and making handles more comfortable to grip, so you can garden in comfort.

### 5. Plant Long-Lasting Flowers

Take a second look at some old favorites. Horticulturists have produced new varieties that flower longer. They include billowing hydrangeas, easy-care lavenders and the versatile, trouble-free Oso Easy Double Red rose from Proven Winners, which continuously blooms from early to late summer.

But if you invest only in one garden tool, make it a long-lasting, well-made pair of shears. They make all the difference in your everyday pruning tasks. Keep them clean and sharp, and you'll be able to deadhead in an instant and also make clean cuts to your shrubs that minimize the risk of damage and disease. Throw in a pruning saw for big jobs, so you won't be tempted to blunt or break your shears on thick stems.

### 3. Pot Bulbs in Layers

Bulbs are self-sufficient, which means you can pack them into pots for spring and summer displays. Try layering a selection of bulbs with different planting depths and staggered flowering times in a container, so you have a continuous, long-lasting show.

### 4. Take the Work Out of Watering

Drought-busting irrigation systems can make watering a breeze instead of a chore, even when you have lots of pots. Link patio plants with a hose-and-dripper system, add an automatic timer to your tap, and sit back and relax, knowing your plants will thrive.

**No. 5**

Plant pretty flowers, like Endless Summer hydrangea, that bloom throughout the growing season.

## 6. Thwart Pests the Natural Way

Garden fabric or netting is a traditional, foolproof way to prevent hungry backyard wildlife from feasting on your homegrown produce. A few clever tools for this include pop-up netting tents and no-fuss covers specifically designed to protect raised veggie beds. And introduce some natural, noninvasive predators, like ladybugs, into the garden. Ladybugs devour huge quantities of pesky aphids. You can buy a legion via mail from specialty suppliers. Release them into your garden at dusk to encourage them to stick around and get to work.

**No. 6**

Weave twigs into natural-looking supports for Euphorbia (pictured) and other plants that need the lift.

*No. 7*

## 7. Support Your Plants

Cane, hoop and ring supports can transform your borders, lifting those floppy stems and preventing plants from dropping over paths. The secret to using plant supports is to get them in early, before the plant puts on too much growth. As the plant thrives, its stems and leaves disguise the support, giving your garden an effortless look of being well-groomed.

## 8. Plant Perennials in Big, Beautiful Drifts

Make a bigger splash with gorgeous flowering perennials by planting them in groups of three, five or even seven. It's much easier to make a natural-looking grouping by arranging odd, rather than even, numbers of plants. Follow recommended planting distances, and the plants soon will grow together to create an exciting mass of color.

## 9. Learn the Secrets of Plant Propagation

Master the art of propagation, and soon your garden will be filled with organically grown plants. Start by sowing the seeds of your favorite flowers. Once they've flowered, let a few plants go to seed. (Be prepared for some surprises if they are hybrids, which don't always come true from seeds.) Then, harvest and store the seeds so they're ready to plant the following year.

## 10. Banish Weeds with Organic Mulch

Lock moisture into your soil and smother out weeds by giving your beds, and even your containers, a thick layer of organic mulch. Use hearty garden compost such as chopped-up leaves, grass clippings without weedkillers, evergreen needles or composted manure for lusher plantings. Plus, your soil will hold water better.

## 11. Deadhead to Keep the Flowers Coming

One of the secrets of spectacular summer flower displays is to pick or snip off dead flower heads regularly. This prevents the plants from setting seed, encouraging them to produce flush after flush of beautiful blooms. Deadhead annuals and most perennials to guarantee a longer season of flowering color from your garden.

## 12. Go Vertical

Maximize your growing space with pocket wall planters. Either fill them with colorful flowers to brighten vertical surfaces or grow salads and leafy herbs, such as basil and parsley. You could add edible flowers, such as nasturtiums or violas, to pep up both your salads and your backyard display.

*No. 13*

## 13. Grow Veggies in Raised Beds

A raised bed kit takes little time to assemble and makes a neat and productive home for your vegetables. Container aficionados will tell you that not only does the soil require less attention, but also fewer weeds will threaten your veggies. Just add a thick layer of garden compost or well-rotted manure whenever the soil is bare, and the worms will take it down into the soil for you.

# Showstopping Shapes

*From hearts to spikes, grow these uncommon forms.* BY RACHAEL LISKA

1

**SQUIRREL DETERRENT**
Crown imperial's foliage has a strong fragrance, which pleases some gardeners, but many dislike it. The good news? The scent keeps squirrels away.

### 1 Crown imperial
*FRITILLARIA IMPERIALIS*, ZONES 5 TO 9

Roll out the red carpet for this exotic-looking royal grower. A crown of lance-shaped foliage and orange, red or yellow bell-shaped flowers sit atop each sturdy stalk in late spring. Mark your calendar as a reminder to plant bulbs in fall so you don't miss the show. **Why we love it:** It's an excellent focal point in a spring garden. Plant it in well-draining soil, full sun or part shade, and in groupings for full effect.

### 2 Blue shrimp plant
*CERINTHE MAJOR* 'PURPURASCENS', ANNUAL

This easy-to-grow plant may look like it's from out of this world, but it's right at home in any garden. Greenish gray foliage and enchanting clusters of bluish purple bracts that surround tubular flowers attract both the pollinators and gardeners alike. **Why we love it:** Blue shrimp plant is great as a filler. Plant it next to purple or bronze-leafed beauties to bring out the complex mix of colors of the bracts.

### 3 Red-hot poker
*KNIPHOFIA UVARIA*, ZONES 5 TO 9

It's easy to see how this sun-loving stunner earned its name. Also called torch flower, its red buds open to tubular orange blooms that fade to yellow. The flamelike shape turns heads in early to late summer.
**Why we love it:** It works well as a focal point in borders and islands, or as a specimen plant in a small-space garden. Hummingbirds like it, too!

**ADD YEAR-ROUND APPEAL** *The unique architecture of these plants doesn't just wow when they're in bloom. Instead of cutting them down in fall, leave some plants to dry, like globe thistle. They keep their form and provide plenty of winter interest.*

### 4 Globe thistle
*ECHINOPS RITRO*, ZONES 3 TO 9

There's much to admire about this perennial that shines in mid- to late summer. Globes in purple and blue hues rise above gray-green foliage on stiff stems, attracting beneficial insects like bees and butterflies. A great addition to a cutting garden, the globes make an impression in both fresh and dried arrangements.
**Why we love it:** Globe thistle has a prickly tough-guy personality. It's low-maintenance and grows well in dry soils, making it perfect for xeriscaping projects.

## 5 Hedgehog agave
*AGAVE STRICTA*,
ZONES 8 TO 10

This hardy succulent from Mexico thrives in western gardens because it's reliably drought-tolerant. Its rosette of spine-tipped evergreen leaves adds a dramatic sculptural element to a rock or xeriscaped garden. When stressed, this agave sometimes turns a lovely shade of pink.

**Why we love it:** Gardeners in cooler climates can try it as an annual in a container. Pair with softer-looking plants for contrast.

## 6 Escargot begonia
*BEGONIA* 'ESCARGOT',
ANNUAL

At first, it may look like something Alice spotted in Wonderland, but this trippy beauty belongs in a partly or fully shaded spot in your backyard. Plant this Rex begonia hybrid in pots where the jaw-dropping, snail-shaped foliage can be viewed and appreciated up close.

**Why we love it:** These begonias require little maintenance—no pruning and deadheading needed. Be sure to avoid overwatering, which tends to invite disease or rot.

## 7 Bleeding heart
*DICENTRA SPECTABILIS*, ZONES 3 TO 9

It may be an old-fashioned favorite, but bleeding heart never goes out of style. Puffy heart-shaped flowers droop from arching stems, giving this low-maintenance plant its name. Blooms fade by summer, so after it flowers, cut it back to encourage new foliage. Place bleeding heart amid plants with a later bloom time.

**Why we love it:** It brightens up shady spots and brings color to woodland gardens with blue-green foliage and fresh pink and white blooms.

**CREATE A WORK OF ART** *Think of your garden as a canvas and these bold, beautiful blooms and leaves as your paints. An informal landscape is the perfect place to experiment with plants in all shapes, sizes and textures to create a masterpiece.*

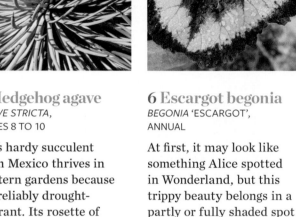

## 8 Fancy-leafed caladium
*CALADIUM X HORTULANUM*, ANNUAL

With amazing color combinations of streaking red, pink, white and green on large heart-shaped leaves, what's not to love about caladium? Pick one variety and plant this shade lover in groups for big impact. Grow caladium as an annual or store tubers indoors during the winter months.

**Why we love it:** Caladium provides vibrant color all season, whether it's planted in containers, along borders or in shady corners.

## 9 Bells of Ireland
*MOLUCCELLA LAEVIS*, ANNUAL

A native from the eastern Mediterranean to India, not Ireland as its name suggests, this showstopper features tiny fragrant white flowers that grow in large green calyxes—protective layers around the petals. The result is breathtaking spikes of blooms that delight from July to September. Plant in full sun for best results.

**Why we love it:** As one of the most interesting cut flowers out there, it takes a simple bouquet of roses or lilies to another level.

### LET THEM SHINE
- Draw even more attention to these nontraditional plants when you grow them in containers near a busy outdoor living space.
- Pair the flashy forms with simple, traditional plants, like ornamental grass or hostas.
- Cut a single bloom to display in a simple bud vase in your home.

## 10 Purple passionflower
*PASSIFLORA INCARNATA*, ZONES 5 TO 9

Get the look of the tropics with these abundant, exotic, unusual blooms that also produce a heady scent. Available in shades of creamy white, blue and purple, this head-turning vine flowers from midsummer through frost and reaches 6 to 10 feet high or more.

**Why we love it:** Its fast-growing, vining habit make it perfect for adorning a trellis or adding privacy to a backyard fence.

## START SMALL

Ground covers are often planted in drifts, or large masses of a single variety, but tiny yards benefit from these low-growers, too. Begin with small drifts of a few species in an empty part of your yard. All of the ground covers shown here, cushion spurge (top), Bugleweed (right) or rock cress (bottom), grow well next to barberry (top right).

# GAINING GROUND

*For a quick fix in hard-to-grow spaces, choose ground covers. Beautiful as well as low-maintenance, they also combat weeds.*

**BY CRYSTAL RENNICKE**

Creeping thyme tolerates light foot traffic—perfect along a stony path.

The average homeowner spends 40 hours a year mowing the lawn. Add time spent trimming, fertilizing and watering, and that glorious green carpet takes a lot of time and effort.

Ground covers are unsung garden heroes that reduce mowing and control weeds. Another perk is an eco-friendly yard that is super attractive to wildlife. Start small with these resilient growers. They take a few years to establish and reduce weeds, but rethinking even one unused area equals less maintenance and work for you.

## Boost Trouble Spots

Ground covers are low-growers that create a living carpet, protect the soil and connect adjacent plants. This group includes everything from horizontally spreading shrubs to vines and perennials.

One tricky area in many gardens is the shady spot underneath shrubs, trees and hedges. Shallow-rooted types, such as spotted deadnettle and variegated common periwinkle (invasive in the eastern U.S.), coexist with the roots of trees and shrubs and crowd out weeds. These plants hold your landscape together, connecting trees and shrubs to other areas.

Ground covers can also be used to hide the foliage of spring bulbs and perennials once they've passed their peak. Plant hostas around daylilies and periwinkles around spring bulbs for attractive vegetation for most of the season. Many varieties produce beautiful colors as the seasons change, and some, like lilyturf and bearberry, produce colorful fruit.

**FILL IN TIGHT SPACES** *The area between rocks and along pathways is a tricky spot to grow anything (other than weeds!), but ground covers such as thyme, moss and hens and chicks thrive in cramped areas.*

Bugleweed grows best in areas with dry shade in Zones 3 to 10.

## SOLVE HOMEOWNER HEADACHES

*For a low-maintenance and resilient garden, try some of these beauties.*

### SLOPES
Dwarf forsythia
Gro-Low fragrant sumac
Daylily

### SHADE
Epimedium
Foam flower
Sedge
Japanese painted fern
Chinese astilbe
Coral bells
Crested iris
Spotted deadnettle
Hosta
Pachysandra

### WET AREAS
Southern blue flag
Umbrella papyrus
Japanese sweet flag
Marsh marigold
Skunk cabbage
Chinese astilbe
Japanese primrose

### BETWEEN STEPPERS
Low-growing thyme
Creeping bugleweed
Sweet alyssum
Corsican pearlwort

### SUNNY SLOPES
Snow in summer
Sedum
Lambs' ears
Big-leaf geranium
Euphorbia
Coreopsis
Dianthus
Candytuft
Lilyturf
Artemisia
Hardy ice plant

### SMALL SPACES
Hens and chicks
Moss phlox
Corydalis
Common thrift
Allegheny foam flower
Chamomile

Bugleweed

Sweet woodruff

# 5 NO-FUSS FILLERS *Perfect for the bare spots in your yard.*

Barrenwort

## Bugleweed
*AJUGA REPTANS* CULTIVARS
ZONES 3 TO 10

**Height:** 3 to 4 inches
**Spread:** Indefinite
**Light needs:** Full sun to part shade
**Landscape uses:** Stone paths or walkways, as it can tolerate light foot traffic.
**Features:** Evergreens with spoon-shaped leaves and variety of colors.

## Barrenwort
*EPIMEDIUM* CULTIVARS
ZONES 4 TO 8, DEPENDING ON CULTIVAR

**Height:** 6 to 16 inches
**Spread:** 1 to 3 feet or more
**Light needs:** Part to full shade
**Landscape uses:** Slow spreader that covers large barren areas. Perfect for shady spots under large trees.
**Features:** Small flowers from mid- to late-spring emerge from red-tinged, heart-shaped leaves on wiry stems.

## Sweet Woodruff
*GALIUM ODORATUM*
ZONES 4 TO 8

**Height:** 6 to 10 inches
**Spread:** Indefinite
**Light needs:** Part to full shade
**Landscape uses:** Spreads under large perennials as well as trees and shrubs.
**Features:** Delicate foliage topped with clusters of fragrant white flowers.

## Foam Flower
*TIARELLA* CULTIVARS
ZONES 3 TO 8

**Height:** 4 to 12 inches
**Spread:** 1 to 1½ feet
**Light needs:** Part shade
**Landscape uses:** Line pathways or arrange in drifts in woodland gardens.
**Features:** Clusters of deeply lobed leaves with wands of tiny white flowers in late spring through the summer season.

Foam flower

Lambs' ears

## Lambs' Ears
*STACHYS BYZANTINA*
ZONES 4 TO 9

**Height:** 4 to 18 inches
**Spread:** 2 to 3 feet
**Light needs:** Grows best in full sun
**Landscape uses:** Informal beds and borders. Makes a great companion plant.
**Features:** Thick woolly leaves topped by spikes of small pinkish-purple flowers.

Instead of mulch, try low-growing varieties such as thyme or bugleweed in flower beds and borders. Once established, these garden helpers protect the soil, so you can skip the mulch each year.

Hard-to-grow, hard-to-mow slopes also benefit from ground covers, which prevent eroding, stop rain from running off and fill in boggy areas.

Finally, for those of you ready to sell the lawn mower, it's possible to have a very low-maintenance lawn. Low-growing thyme, snow in summer or moss are pretty lawn substitutes. As an added benefit, your water bill may decrease—lawn grass requires two to four times more water than ground covers.

### Choose Your Plants
Before you head to the garden center, familiarize yourself with your growing conditions. Have your soil tested to identify which plants thrive best in your yard, and observe how much sunlight the area receives. While many ground covers are adaptable, matching the plant to the sun conditions right off the bat helps assure success.

You may be tempted to choose the most colorful and florific plants, but first select varieties with leaves that are attractive all season or year-round. Consider other features like flowers or berries to be bonuses. Leaves are available in a variety of textures and colors, and variegated kinds range from all shades of green to pinks and yellows.

Also beware of size. Ground covers can grow anywhere from 1 inch to 4 feet, so height is key in plant selection. Steer clear of a tall fern that blocks your perennials, and consider lambs' ears to use between your lawn grass and flower beds.

Next, select plants that spread with similar speeds. Really

vigorous growers are not ideal near less vigorous ones—they'll end up claiming the entire bed and will require more work. Choose other plants that cover at the same rate.

Spreading type also affects growth. Some, like bugleweed, spread indefinitely, but because of its shallow roots, it's easy to control. Bishop's weed, on the other hand, spreads by rhizomes that are almost impossible to keep in bounds.

If you do end up with one plant that seems to be spreading too fast, dig it up or take out any nearby plants to give that one more space.

As with most plant categories, some grow beyond their bounds. Beware of and take care not to plant invasives, such as English ivy, kudzu, Japanese honeysuckle, wintercreeper, crown vetch and creeping Jenny.

### Ready, Set, Enjoy
After you've chosen a space, prepare it by removing the vegetation. Loosen the soil 6 to 8 inches down, and add 2 to 3 inches of compost or organic material. When working near trees, there's no need to add soil or deeply cultivate; it may injure the plants.

Check spacing requirements. You may be tempted to plant closely to fill in gaps, but this could crowd them and lead to disease. Instead of making tidy rows, stagger plants to make them appear natural. Dig a hole deep enough for the roots, pat down and water thoroughly. (Watering is key in the first few years.) Spread a layer of mulch between the plants to keep any weeds out.

Once plants are established in good soil, an occasional cultivation of weeds and pruning keeps ground covers healthy and in check.

# Bloom-tastic Trees

*Celebrate the season with one of these special specimens, most of them sized perfectly for small spaces.*   BY DEB WILEY

**1**

**PLANT PINK**
Crabapples make great nesting trees for chipping sparrows, and they also are host plants for io moth larvae.

### 1 Flowering crabapple

*MALUS*, ZONES 4 TO 8
SIZE: 6 TO 8 FEET TALL AND
WIDE TO 20 TO 25 FEET TALL
AND WIDE

Crabapples are the darlings of cool-climate yards. Flowers of white, pink or deep crimson transform into dainty fruits in yellow, orange, maroon or red. Select a newer variety to ensure good disease- and pest-resistance, and plant in full sun.
**Why we love it:** The diversity! Tree shapes can be rounded, spreading, upright, vase shaped and even weeping.

### 2 Magnolia

*MAGNOLIA*, ZONES 4 TO 9
SIZE: 15 TO 40 FEET TALL
AND WIDE

Gorgeous blooms in white, pink, yellow and purple balance like teacups or starbursts atop branches that later bear green leaves, some as glossy as lacquer. Plant in full sun to part shade.
**Why we love it:** There's one for almost every region, from star magnolia (*Magnolia stellata*) in the chilly north to southern and champaca magnolias in the balmy south, and saucer magnolias everywhere in between.

### 3 Carolina silverbell

*HALESIA TETRAPTERA* (OR *HALESIA CAROLINA*), ZONES 4 TO 8
SIZE: 30 TO 40 FEET TALL, 20 TO 35 FEET WIDE

Almost maintenance-free and able to grow in full sun to full shade, keep Carolina silverbell moist and in well-draining, acidic soil. Test your soil for a pH below 7.
**Why we love it:** Children and adults alike might believe that fairies come by to ring its elegant white or rose bell-shaped blossoms.

**THE CARE AND KEEPING OF TREES** *Replace all of the grass that surrounds freshly planted and young trees with mulch. Grass is a fierce competitor for water and other nutrients, and it can drastically slow the growth of your tree.*

### 4 Japanese tree lilac

*SYRINGA RETICULATA* SSP. *RETICULATA*,
ZONES 3 TO 7
SIZE: 20 TO 30 FEET TALL, 15 TO 25 FEET WIDE

Flowering a bit later than other lilacs, this underused tree releases a sweet scent from its cone-shaped panicles of ivory blooms. Sorry southerners, but this is a cold-climate choice. Plant it in full sun.
**Why we love it:** It's unusual and grows even in the most difficult places such as highway medians.

## 5 Yellowwood
*CLADRASTIS KENTUKEA,*
ZONES 4 TO 8
SIZE: 30 TO 50 FEET TALL
AND SLIGHTLY WIDER

Yellowwood's best bloom show occurs every other year, when you're treated to cascading 8- to 14-inch sprays of delicate, fragrant white blossoms. Grow it in full sun. If you live in areas of heavy snow, beware of branches that snap off in winter.
**Why we love it:** This is a blooming shade tree that has bark like a beech tree, providing winter interest.

## 6 Apple serviceberry
*AMELANCHIER X GRANDIFLORA,*
ZONES 4 TO 9
SIZE: 20 TO 25 FEET TALL AND WIDE

Apple serviceberry is just one kind of serviceberry that's perfect for most landscapes, thanks to its moderate size, bird-attracting berries and ability to thrive in sun to part sun locations.
**Why we love it:** It's a special tree with four seasons of beauty: spring blooms that become red-purple edible fruits, green leaves that flush with orange to red fall color, and smooth silver bark that's gorgeous in winter.

## 7 Eastern redbud
*CERCIS CANADENSIS,* ZONES 4 TO 9
SIZE: 20 TO 30 FEET TALL, 25 TO 35 FEET WIDE

Dainty rose-purple blooms dramatically hang from the branches of this North American native well before the heart-shaped leaves appear. Plant in full sun to part shade.
**Why we love it:** The small size fits most yards. You can select alternate leaf colors, such as burgundy Forest Pansy or lime-gold The Rising Sun.

**ROOM TO GROW** *Plant your eastern redbud tree in a spot where it has space to spread out, because this spring showstopper is wider than it is tall.*

## 8 Japanese flowering cherry
*PRUNUS SERRULATA,* ZONES 5 TO 8
SIZE: 40 TO 50 FEET TALL AND 25 TO 40 FEET WIDE

You might *ooh* and *aah* every spring at the photos of the cherry tree display in Washington, D.C., but you can plant a flowering show of your own. Choose a spot in full sun.
**Why we love it:** With the right cultivar, those gorgeous pink or white blooms turn into fruits that birds—especially robins, cardinals and waxwings—crave.

## 9 Dogwood

**CORNUS KOUSA**, ZONES 5 TO 8; CORNUS
FLORIDA, ZONES 5 TO 9
SIZE: 20 TO 40 FEET TALL AND WIDE

Flowers up to 4 inches wide grace
the spring branches of North
American and Asian dogwoods.
Test your soil pH before planting
because dogwood grows best
planted in acidic soil in full sun
to full shade.

**Why we love it:** In addition to
the graceful spring flowers and fall
leaf colors, the colorful red fruits
produced by dogwood are gobbled
up by feathered friends.

---

**LATE BLOOMERS**
*These uncommon flowering
trees wait until summer to
unfurl their signature look.*

- **JAPANESE STEWARTIA**
  (*Stewartia pseudocamellia*):
  "Camellia" in its botanical
  name says something about
  the flowers. Zones 5 to 8.
- **SOURWOOD** (*Oxydendrum
  arboreum*): Tiny, fragrant,
  white bell-shaped flowers
  hang in cone-shaped clusters.
  Zones 5 to 9.
- **KOREAN EVODIA**
  (*Tetradium daniellii*): It's also
  called the bee tree, thanks
  to small white blossoms on
  female plants. Zones 4 to 8.

---

## 10 White fringe tree

**CHIONANTHUS VIRGINICUS**, ZONES 4 TO 9
SIZE: 12 TO 20 FEET TALL AND WIDE

Native ranging from southern
Pennsylvania south to Florida and
west to Texas, fringe tree bursts
onto the spring scene with lightly
fragrant strappy white petals.
They're held in small groups
attached at the top like tassels.

**Why we love it:** It's the best-kept
secret among spring-blooming
trees, yet it's one of the most
adaptable, thriving in full sun to
part shade. Female trees produce
blue fruits that birds love.

# love *your* lawn

*The grass is always greener (and your backyard birds happier)*
*when you follow this advice from a pro.*  BY MELINDA MYERS

I**N A PERFECT WORLD**, your grass is healthy, green and pesticide-free. It's a safe haven where birds linger, butterflies flutter and children run and play. The ideal lawn is a lush backdrop for flowerbeds and home base for summer get-togethers. Fortunately, the lawn of your dreams is within reach.

Success for any lawn starts with the soil. Most lawns and landscapes are planted in soil that is less than ideal. When houses are built, the rich topsoil is scraped off and carted away, leaving compacted soil full of rocks and debris. What's left is a problematic foundation for growing grass, trees and most plants. That's why it's crucial to mix several inches of compost into the top 8 inches of soil before planting grass. If you're dealing with an existing lawn and aren't willing to rip it out and start over, there are other steps you can take.

Begin to repair the damage and improve the growing conditions by core aerating your current lawn. This process removes plugs of soil, reduces compaction and creates openings for air, water and nutrients to reach the roots. Fall is the best time for northern gardeners to aerate, while spring or early summer is ideal for those in the South.

In addition to creating a strong foundation, ongoing care is needed to keep a lawn healthy and happy. That care includes three major tasks: mowing, fertilizing and watering.

**WATER-WISE**
When in doubt, skip the sprinkle. Most turf grasses can endure an occasional dry spell in the heat of the summer months.

## 4 WAYS TO A LASTING LAWN

- **Sharpen the mower's blade.**
  You'll use less gasoline, the plants retain more moisture and you reduce their risk of disease.
- **Use a manual push mower.**
  Burn calories and eliminate carbon emissions at the same time.
- **Go no mow.**
  Create a meadowlike look with fine fescue lawns. Or cut fescue once a month for a more traditional look.
- **Convert to a clover lawn.**
  It's drought tolerant, and pollinators love that clover.

Be sure to mow high and often, and leave the clippings. The taller the grass, the deeper the roots, which makes lawns better able to tolerate drought and crowd out weeds.

When mowing, remove no more than one-third the total height of the grass. It is less stressful on the lawn, and the short clippings break down quickly to add moisture, nutrients and organic matter to the soil. Keep this in mind: A season's worth of clippings equals one fertilizer application. So get rid of the bagger and enjoy this added benefit.

When it comes to adding fertilizer, there's a right way to go about it. Apply at least once a year to reduce the weeds. Add a second or third application to increase the health and density of your lawn and further crowd out weeds. The best choice is a slow-release organic fertilizer because it provides a steady stream of nutrients.

Northern gardeners who grow cool-season grasses should fertilize at least once in the fall, around Halloween, before the ground freezes. But for a more robust lawn, also apply on Memorial Day and Labor Day. (Use holidays to help you remember when to apply!) Warm-season grasses that are grown in southern regions should be fertilized around Easter, after the grass starts growing. Add Memorial Day and Labor Day to beef up lawn performance. For gardeners in the South, make sure the last fall application is at least one month before the average first killing frost.

## IDEAL HEIGHTS FOR COMMON LAWNS

**COOL-SEASON GRASS**

- Bluegrass: 3 to 3½ inches
- Fescue: 3 to 3½ inches
- Perennial ryegrass: 3 to 3½ inches

**WARM-SEASON GRASS**

- Zoysia: 2 inches
- Bermuda: 2 inches
- Carpet: 2 inches
- Centipede: 2 inches
- St. Augustine: 3 inches

Weeds are probably the greatest source of frustration for you and your neighbors. When it comes to a healthy lawn, you may need to tolerate a few weeds. Clover is considered a weed, but now it's also gaining popularity as a fast-growing grass substitute. It's great for the bees, and it helps nurture your lawn. It was once added to grass seed mixtures to boost growth. Clover's benefit is pulling nitrogen out of the atmosphere and adding it to the soil. You might even find the rabbits eating clover instead of your hostas.

And then there are dandelions, the ultimate pest to some, but an asset to others. Dandelions are edible, make a great wine, are high in vitamin C and attract a wide range of pollinators. If you're not ready to tolerate these invaders, try an eco-friendly solution. Break out the dandelion digger, weed knife or your favorite tool and remove unwanted weeds, roots and all. If this doesn't work, treat individual plants and problem areas. You'll use less weed killer, plus it's better for the environment and your pocketbook.

Make a few of these changes and soon your lush and healthy lawn will be a haven for both you and your favorite wildlife.

Water is important to all plants, but irrigated lawns are water guzzlers. Reduce watering with drought-tolerant grasses, like buffalo, that are suited to your climate, and allow your lawn to go dormant during dry weather. A healthy lawn suited to the local climate usually tolerates typical summer droughts. Consider it a welcome break from mowing, but be prepared to pull a few more weeds. Those pesky growers seem to survive and thrive in these adverse conditions.

**THINK OUTSIDE THE LAWN** *All plants, including lawns, provide benefits for wildlife and pollinators. The grass in your landscape cools our environment, absorbs storm water, reduces soil erosion and produces oxygen.*

# Sweet Summer Aromas

*Grow perennial powerhouses that will convince you to stop and smell the flowers. Bonus! Pollinators love them.* **BY RACHAEL LISKA**

1

**BUTTERFLY BONUS**
The Stargazer lily offers a fragrant treat for your nose and attracts butterflies, too!

### 1 Oriental lily
*LILIUM ORIENTALIS*
ZONES 4 TO 9
SIZE: 2 TO 5 FEET HIGH

Sound the horn for these trumpet-shaped blooms that smell as exotic as they look. For easy color in the garden, lilies are No. 1. The trouble is in deciding which gorgeous variety to grow. Just be sure to provide a little extra staking for when summer storms blow in. **Why we love it:** There's no need to visit a florist with bouquet-ready beauties growing in your backyard. Remove faded flowers to direct energy into the bulbs for next year's floral display.

### 2 Bee balm
*MONARDA*, ZONES 4 TO 9
SIZE: 2 TO 4 FEET HIGH

These cheery plants with funky hairdos are native to North America. With spiky, daisylike blooms in red, blue, violet, white or pink hues, bee balm, as its name suggests, is a pollinator magnet. Its aroma is similar to oregano but contains some hints of citrus, mint and thyme. **Why we love it:** Bee balm attracts butterflies, hummingbirds and bees, but not usually deer—so it's a smart bet if you live in a wooded area with a large population of these garden grazers.

### 3 Lily-of-the-valley
*CONVALLARIA MAJUS*, ZONES 3 TO 9
SIZE: 4 TO 8 INCHES HIGH AND WIDE

Dainty white blossoms sitting on lush green foliage may catch the eye first, but if you get a little closer, lily-of-the-valley's sweet scent lures you in. Blooming in spring through early summer, this perennial favorite can brighten up your garden's shady spots. Before you plant it, make sure it's not invasive in your area.
**Why we love it:** The small stature and spreading growth habit makes it an excellent ground cover option.

---

**THE SCIENCE BEHIND THE SCENT** *Essential oils in the petals of most plants produce fragrances, but it's not just to appease your nose. When flowers give off their unique smells, it's an alert to pollinators that they are ready for pollination.*

---

### 4 Garden phlox
*PHLOX PANICULATA*, ZONES 3 TO 9
SIZE: 2 TO 5 FEET HIGH, 1 TO 3 FEET WIDE

Found naturally in forests, in open fields and clinging to cliff walls, this hardy perennial with a heady fragrance offers many disease-resistant varieties to choose from. Bloom colors run the gamut from red, pink and rose to lavender, deep purple, white and even bicolor.
**Why we love it:** Phlox is a showstopper in a summer garden, and it blooms for six weeks or more. Plus, it's known to attract hummingbirds.

### 5 Sweet autumn clematis
*CLEMATIS TERNIFLORA*
ZONES 4 TO 9
SIZE: 10 TO 15 FEET HIGH

This vigorous perennial vine features fluffy clouds of fragrant, creamy white flowers that spill romantically over fences, arbors or pergolas—even in partial shade. Keep its aggressive nature in check by pruning in spring before growth begins.
**Why we love it:** As other flowers fade in late summer, sweet autumn clematis starts its show and goes through fall.

### 6 English lavender
*LAVANDULA ANGUSTIFOLIA*
ZONES 5 TO 10
SIZE: 12 TO 14 INCHES HIGH, 12 TO 16 INCHES WIDE

A forever favorite, lavender is prized for intensely fragrant purple-blue blooms that can be cut and displayed in floral arrangements or dried to use in teas, spice mixes or potpourris. Pollinators such as butterflies and bees can't resist lavender's intoxicating lure.
**Why we love it:** This sun lover thrives in well-draining soils and looks lovely season after season.

### 7 Cottage pinks
*DIANTHUS PLUMARIUS*, ZONES 3 TO 10
SIZE: 12 TO 18 INCHES HIGH AND WIDE

Pinks are an old-fashioned favorite, thanks to their nose-turning bouquet of cinnamon and warm clove. Small fringed flowers of white, pink and red sit above slender foliage that puts on spring and summer shows. Plant cottage pinks in full sun, and deadhead promptly for best results.
**Why we love it:** This plant is incredibly versatile. From containers to border displays to rock gardens, cottage pinks look lovely wherever you plant them.

**DISAPPEARING ACT** *Many popular plants are bred to maximize color, shape or petals, or to produce long-lasting flowers. Extensive breeding often causes the scents to diminish, which is why new hybrid varieties are not as wildlife-friendly as natives.*

Sarah Bernhardt peony

### 8 Common peony
*PAEONIA LACTIFLORA*, ZONES 3 TO 8
SIZE: 2½ TO 3 FEET HIGH AND WIDE

Its large, showy cup-shaped flowers can't be beat, but the easy-to-grow peony also has sturdy stems that won't need staking and tons of fragrance. For ultimate aromatherapy, choose a cultivar prized for its scent, such as Festiva Maxima, Sarah Bernhardt, or Eden's Perfume.
**Why we love it:** Peonies are reliable performers that offer big impact without a lot of work. Their show is brief, but it's nothing short of spectacular.

## 9 Rose

*ROSA*, ZONES 3 TO 10
SIZE: 1 TO 15 FEET HIGH,
UP TO 8 FEET WIDE

With scents including apple, melon, honey, orange and even wine, these beauties make you stop to take them in. For that classic rose aroma, opt for English, floribunda, heirloom or antique varieties such as Honey Perfume, Heritage, and Louise Odier.

**Why we love it:** With so many colors available, it's easy to find a rose to suit your nose. Plus, it's hardy!

### GET MORE FROM YOUR FRAGRANT FAVORITES

- Create an aromatic container garden on a patio or terrace.
- Plant these pleasant-smelling beauties near a window or the front door.
- Grow scented herbs. Rosemary, mint and basil do double duty in the kitchen.

## 10 Sage

*SALVIA NEMOROSA*, ZONES 4 TO 8
SIZE: 1 TO 2 FEET HIGH AND WIDE

Sage is drought-tolerant and easy to grow. It makes a stunning cut flower and attracts hummingbirds, butterflies and bees. Plus, the foliage is wonderfully fragrant. If you're short on space, try a small cultivar like Blue Hill.

**Why we love it:** Less watering means less work (and more time to enjoy summer on the patio). Mother Nature will thank you, too!

# Trim Back for Bonus Blooms

*One pinch and poof! Your faded flowers get fresh new life.* **BY NIKI JABBOUR**

Deadheading may sound strange, but it's actually a super-easy technique that has a big effect on the health and appearance of your garden. When a plant flowers and sets seed, it stops producing fresh blossoms. Simply put, deadheading is the practice of removing faded or dead flowers *before* they go to seed, so that new ones are encouraged to grow.

Horticulturist Jessica Walliser says that it's an essential summer chore if you want to keep your garden looking its best, but it is good practice any time you have fading blooms in your containers and garden beds.

Both annuals and perennials benefit from regular trimming back.

Flowering annuals, like zinnias, cosmos and petunias, respond by pumping out fresh blooms from spring through autumn. This technique also prolongs the flowering period of certain perennial plants, like foxglove, rose and lavender. "Perennials that produce many flowers throughout the growing season continue to generate more blooms with deadheading," says Jessica, adding that side buds develop second and even third flushes of blooms. Your best bets for reblooming include Shasta daisy, bee balm, salvia, yarrow and coneflower.

Besides kicking off bonus blooms, snipping away any faded flowers prevents the unwanted spread of vigorous self-seeding annuals and perennials, like poppy, columbine and globe thistle. All you have to do is pinch off the spent blooms of self-seeders before they set and spread their seeds all over your garden. Producing seeds drains a plant's energy, too, so deadheading before seed heads start to weigh down the plant's foliage will help keep it growing longer and looking its very best.

Deadheading is also the perfect opportunity to take a closer look at your plants, so you can spot any early warning signs of disease. Leaves and stems hidden from view are usually the first to show symptoms.

But before you grab your gardening shears, make sure you know the right way to get rid of faded flowers. Proper deadheading removes the entire flower head. With a quick pinch of the fingers or small pruning shears, snip the stem, either back to a new flower bud or fresh side branch growth. If you

**SKIP THE SHEARS!**
If you find deadheading to be tedious, look for annual and perennial plants that don't need it. Supertunia petunias, nemesia, astilbe and baptisia are some of the good options.

only snip off the petals but leave the immature seed pod behind, your flowers won't rebloom. Just be careful not to remove any flowering side shoots. And if your plant produces individual flowers in one cluster, like daylilies, wait until most of the blooms fade before removing the flowering stem.

Make sure to keep up with deadheading so that it doesn't become a huge chore you need to tackle all at once later on. Depending on the size of your garden, plucking fading blooms should be an easy task that takes only a few minutes.

So, not only will deadheading leave your containers and gardens looking tidy, but it will keep your flowers looking fresh and healthy.

---

## THE BEST BLOOMS FOR DEADHEADING
*These plants are strong performers when you yank their faded flowers.*

| | | |
|---|---|---|
| Bee balm | Hollyhock | Salvia |
| Butterfly weed | Lavender | Shasta daisy |
| Columbine | Marigold | Speedwell |
| Cosmos | Monkshood | Yarrow |
| Garden phlox | Rose campion | |

# Spice Up Your Butterfly Garden

*Grow gorgeous annuals from easy-to-find seeds.*  BY SALLY ROTH

**FOR THE BIRDS**
Butterflies and pollinators can't get enough of fennel blooms, but warblers and other songbirds love the seeds, too!

1

### 1 Fennel
*FOENICULUM VULGARE*

A culinary old-timer that's been around since Spaniards brought seeds to California 200 years ago, fennel is a fast-growing herb that adds delicacy and height to flowerbeds. It reaches up to 3 feet tall and has abundant clusters of tiny, buttery yellow flowers.
**Why we love it:** Many butterfly species, including black and anise swallowtails, flock to fennel both for its nectar and to use it as a host plant for their very hungry caterpillars.

### 2 Caraway
*CARUM CARVI*

Eat a rye bread sandwich and you'll see (and taste!) savory caraway seeds. The crescent-shaped seeds are produced by a plant that looks a lot like Queen Anne's lace, thanks to its clusters of tiny white and pinkish flowers. This biennial reaches 2 feet tall and may not flower until its second year.
**Why we love it:** As a host plant, it's fantastic for black swallowtail eggs, while yellow-green sulphurs and metalmark butterflies stop by to snack on its nectar.

### 3 Nigella
*NIGELLA SATIVA*

Blue blossoms backed by a ruff of fine leaves make this flower look extraterrestrial, and butterflies can't get enough of it. Shake the oversize pods to harvest abundant black seeds for use in Indian or South Asian dishes.
**Why we love it:** Butterflies of all shapes and sizes, including sulphurs, whites, fritillaries and coppers, are attracted to nigella.

**TIPS FOR SOWING SEED** *Scatter the seeds in a sunny spot in early spring, cover lightly with soil and keep moist until they sprout. If you decide to try planting seeds from the kitchen, sow thickly to make up for any potential duds and increase the odds of success.*

### 4 Cumin
*CUMINUM CYMINUM*

With delicate white bloom bursts, cumin looks like a smaller, daintier cousin of Queen Anne's lace. The ridged seeds grow into branching annuals that stand 18 inches tall. Soak seeds overnight before planting for faster germination.
**Why we love it:** Blues, hairstreaks, sulphurs and many other small to medium-size butterflies love to land on the flowers.

### 5 Chia
*SALVIA HISPANICA*

If you loved your chia pet, grow one in the garden. Chia seeds come from salvia, a plant native to Mexico. Enjoy sky blue flowers as well as the nutritional benefits of these ancient seeds, which are great in smoothies. Plant seeds outside in fall in Zones 9 to 11. In colder regions, start them in pots indoors in late winter.
**Why we love it:** Monarchs, painted ladies and red admirals adore this oh-so lovely flower.

### 6 Anise
*PIMPINELLA ANISUM*

Blanketed in snowy white clusters, anise is a tall annual that reaches 3 feet high. The feathery plants are an airy presence in the garden, and their star-shaped seeds have a licorice-like taste and aroma.
**Why we love it:** Swallowtails of every sort, such as two-tailed and pipevine, can't get enough of its light and delicate flower clusters. It's also a host plant for black swallowtail and anise swallowtail.

### 7 Sesame
*SESAMUM INDICUM*

Humans have been using sesame seeds for more than 4,000 years, making it the oldest known oil crop. This robust and drought-tolerant plant has tubular flowers that resemble foxglove blossoms and dangle from leafy stems that can reach up to 3 feet. It thrives best in areas with long, hot summers.
**Why we love it:** Sesame flowers can self-pollinate, but they still produce sweet nectar to tempt wandering pollinators such as butterflies and bees. Monarchs and fritillaries visit, as do sphinx moths and hummingbirds. Honeybees also love sesame's tempting blooms.

**SEEDKEEPER SECRETS** *As an experiment, try growing these plants straight from your spice rack! Use organic whole seed, rather than ground or powdered spices. Their ability to sprout will also depend on how they've been stored and processed.*

### 8 Dill
*ANETHUM GRAVEOLENS*

This annual adds appealing contrasts of color and texture to flowerbeds, thanks to feathery fronds and bright yellow flowers. And dill seeds give the popular pickles their tasty zing.
**Why we love it:** Not only is dill irresistible to anglewings, tortoiseshells and sulphurs, but it's also a favorite host plant of black swallowtails.

## 9 Mustard Seed
*SINAPSIS ALBA*

Mustard seeds are quick to grow into vigorous, long-blooming plants that stand 2 feet tall. Prolific stems topped with saffron-yellow flowers hold a passing butterfly's attention for many minutes—long enough for you to grab your camera and snap a photo.

**Why we love it:** Every nectar-sipping butterfly in the area, from the tiniest of blues to big swallowtails and monarchs, enjoys this buttery yellow annual. It's also a host plant for cabbage white and checkered white species.

**CATERPILLAR CARE**
The foliage of dill, anise, fennel and other members of the carrot family is a popular place for swallowtails to lay eggs because the leaves are nourishing for ravenous caterpillars.

## 10 Coriander
*CORIANDRUM SATIVUM*

This beloved favorite has a split personality. Its round seeds are common in Indian cuisine, but its fresh leaves are what we know as cilantro. Clusters of delicate white, pinkish or pale lavender flowers top these 2-foot annuals. From New England to Montana, naturalized coriander grows across the United States.

**Why we love it:** Small to medium-sized butterflies, like hairstreaks, sulphurs, metalmarks and blues, flutter to it.

# The
# Plant Doctor
## Is In!

*Some women get flowers;
I get bags of insects and dead and
diseased plants. But I love it.
During my travels to garden shows
around the country, I connect
with thousands of gardeners,
field their burning backyard
questions and offer diagnoses.
Here are six of the most common
questions they ask.*

**BY MELINDA MYERS**

**1**

## HOW OFTEN SHOULD I WATER INDOOR PLANTS?

This probably isn't the answer you want to hear: It depends. The amount of water a plant needs is based on type, light exposure, potting mix, temperature and humidity. If your house is warm and you're growing a tropical plant in a sunny window, you need to water more often than someone who keeps a cool house and has less light.

When in doubt, test the moisture level by sticking your finger into the top inch or two of potting mix. Cacti and succulents like to go a bit drier, while tropical plants prefer consistently moist, not wet, soil. Pour off excess water that collects in the saucer beneath the planter to prevent root rot.

**Rx**
To save time and increase humidity around plants, place flat pebbles in the saucer under your pot.

## ② WHAT'S WRONG WITH MY PLANT?

I see this question every time I open my email inbox. First, identify the plant and get to know its ideal growing conditions and common ailments. Make sure you've got the preferred soil and are providing the right amounts of water and sun. Next, do an internet search for insect and disease problems common to the plant. Local university and botanical garden websites are your best online resources. If the problem is cosmetic and won't compromise the plant's health, you may want to live with it, since the plant can. But if the plant's health is in danger and you want to save it, use the most eco-friendly option available.

**Rx**
Grow purple-leafed ninebark (shown here) in full sun with good airflow to keep the plants thriving.

## ③ WHAT IS THIS PLANT?

Make plant ID easier for yourself, or whomever you enlist to help, with basic information about the subject, such as age, size, growth habit and bloom time. If possible, take close-up pictures of the leaves, stems and flowers and then the whole plant. Or take a physical sample to your local garden center or extension office. Make sure the leaves and, if present, flowers are attached. All these clues lead to a quicker and more accurate plant identification.

## 4 WHERE DID THE HOLES IN MY HOSTAS COME FROM?

Slugs are the main culprits, but earwigs, hail, frost and even falling maple seeds pierce leaves. Slugs and earwigs prefer the cool, dark locations that hostas thrive in. There's an easy remedy, though. Sink a shallow can filled with beer near the hostas, or set a half-empty beer bottle on its side in the hosta area of the garden. Attracted to the fermenting yeast, the slugs crawl into the container and die.

You can set a trap for earwigs. Place a piece of crumpled paper under an overturned flowerpot overnight. In the morning, lift the pot and shake the paper over a can of soapy water. This is a natural way to check for, and control, backyard earwig populations.

## 5 IS IT A WEED OR A FLOWER?

First, keep in mind that a weed is just a plant out of place. Even good plants are deemed weeds if they're unwanted in your garden. If a mystery plant fits any or all of these descriptions, you may have a weed on your hands:

- It's multiplied considerably since last year.
- It's sprouted up throughout the bed and surrounding lawn.
- It has been in the garden for a few years, never seems to bloom and has unimpressive foliage. (But remember: Perennials and biennials do not bloom in the first summer, and some plants need a few years to establish and flower.)
- You don't like it. Once you decide a plant must go, keep the aggressive ones out of your compost pile or they will return. Dispose of them as recommended by your municipality. If it's just a matter of taste, find a gardener willing to take an ugly duckling off your hands.

Look for nonseeding varieties of invasive plants, like this Lo and Behold, a variety of butterfly bush.

## 6 WHY IS THERE WHITE POWDER ON MY PLANT'S LEAVES?

It's a fungal disease called powdery mildew. Over time, it blocks sunlight, causing foliage to turn yellow and, in severe cases, drop off. Fortunately, this disease doesn't usually kill healthy plants, though it does affect appearance and reduce vegetable productivity.

If this disease is an annual problem in your garden, it may be time to take action. Plant something a bit shorter in front of the susceptible specimen. The shorter plant masks the unsightly mildewed leaves but allows you to enjoy the blossoms. If you want to take a more aggressive course of action, organic products are available. Do a thorough cleanup and discard infected leaves in fall to reduce the source of disease next year. Stop powdery mildew before it starts by choosing mildew-resistant varieties whenever possible. Give plants plenty of room and sunlight; sufficient light and airflow reduce the risk of the disease.

Leaves infected with powdery mildew look as if they've been dusted with flour.

# The No. 1 Weed

*Surprisingly nutritious and tasty, dandelions have unexpected benefits. Read up before you yank 'em.* **BY KAITLIN STAINBROOK**

**19**

**A DANDY DRINK**

*Pharmacists in 19th-century England made tea from roasted dandelion roots. The drink is still trendy today, thanks to a coffeelike taste and color without caffeine.*

**112** A cup of chopped raw dandelion greens provides 112 percent of the daily requirement for vitamin A (at only 25 calories).

**1957**

Ray Bradbury's 1957 novel *Dandelion Wine* gets its title from the wine the characters make and drink in summer.

**300** *A single dandelion* head consists of up to 300 ray flowers that look like tiny petals at first glance.

**1,620**

Dandelions are part of the daisy family, one of the biggest in botany with more than 1,620 genera of plant types.

**24** *Dandelion flowers reach* heights of 6 to 24 inches, and roots go as deep as 10 to 15 feet.

**100** From blossom to root, 100 percent of this weed, which is also an herb, is edible for most people.

# Tiny Trees, Please!

*For evergreen textures and major bird appeal, grow these petite yet pretty conifers.* **BY MELINDA MYERS**

**1**

**GIVE 'EM TIME**
It takes a few years for seeds to develop and nestle in the cones, but in the meantime, birds use the trees as shelter from harsh weather and predators.

### 1 Japanese cedar
*CRYPTOMERIA JAPONICA*
'ELEGANS NANA', ZONES 5 TO 8
SIZE: 4 TO 6 FEET TALL AND WIDE

The soft, feathery texture of tiered branches creates an appealing overall irregular shape. Grow it in moist, rich, fertile soil and full sun. Japanese cedar tolerates light shade and actually appreciates a little afternoon shade.
**Why we love it:** The unusual shape combined with blue-green summer foliage and bronzy-purple winter color makes it a star in all seasons.

### 2 Bright Gold yew
*TAXUS CUPIDATA* 'BRIGHT GOLD',
ZONES 4 TO 7
SIZE: 3 FEET TALL AND WIDE

Add a splash of sunshine to your spring landscape with the golden needles of Bright Gold. Grow it in full sun with a little afternoon shade for the best color. Needles eventually fade to bright green as the season progresses. It tolerates urban conditions but needs moist, well-draining soil and protection from cold winter winds.
**Why we love it:** Relish its naturally small scale, or prune it to fit your space.

### 3 Weeping blue atlas cedar
*CEDRUS ATLANTICA* 'GLAUCA PENDULA', ZONES 6 TO 9
SIZE: VARIABLE

Sculpt this pliable beauty into a curtain, fountain or carpet of blue-green foliage that fits your space and landscape design. Train the main stem and prune the tree to create a one-of-a-kind focal point. Grow this gem in full sun or partial shade with moist, well-draining soil in a spot with protection from strong winds.
**Why we love it:** The swooping branches covered in bluish-green needles look like water cascading over stones.

---

**GOOD THINGS COME IN SMALL PACKAGES** *Whether your space is itty-bitty or super spacious, these terrific trees add year-round interest and come in countless sizes, shapes and foliage colors. Find one that's a perfect fit for your backyard.*

---

ideal for rock gardens

### 4 Blue Shag pine
*PINUS STROBUS* 'BLUE SHAG', ZONES 3 TO 8
SIZE: 2 TO 4 FEET TALL AND 2 TO 5 FEET WIDE

This pine's short, soft needles are dusted with a tinge of blue. You'll need to practice patience, though, because birds won't find cones until the plants start to mature. This gem thrives in average, well-draining soil and full sun but tolerates partial shade. Grow it in acidic soils and pollution-free areas for best results.
**Why we love it:** Its texture, color and density make it a perfect addition to rock gardens.

### 5 Dwarf globe blue spruce

*PICEA PUNGENS* 'GLAUCA GLOBOSA', ZONES 2 TO 7
SIZE: 3 TO 5 FEET TALL AND 4 TO 6 FEET WIDE

Plant this low-maintenance evergreen in full sun. Water it regularly while it's young, but once it's established, give it a good soak during dry periods. It adapts to most soils and tolerates air pollution and even some shade. Watch as new growth emerges a vibrant blue-green in spring.
**Why we love it:** Stiff needles offer birds excellent protection from predators.

### 6 Blueberry Delight juniper

*JUNIPERUS COMMUNIS* 'BLUEBERRY DELIGHT', ZONES 3 TO 7
SIZE: 1 TO 2 FEET TALL AND 4 TO 5 FEET WIDE

The silver, striped needles on this North American native appear powdery blue, making it a standout in the garden. In fall, the needles transform into a beautiful coppery bronze color. It's tolerant of full sun, cold winters and, once established, drought.
**Why we love it:** Bird activity picks up during cooler months as feathered friends flock to feast on the abundant blueberry-like fleshy cones.

### 7 Dwarf Golden arborvitae

*THUJA ORIENTALIS* 'AUREA NANA', ZONES 6 TO 9
SIZE: 2 TO 6 FEET TALL AND 2 TO 5 FEET WIDE

The name may have changed (it's sometimes known as *Platycladus orientalis* 'Aurea Nana'), but its mass appeal remains. The pointed globe of golden-yellow foliage turns bronzy in winter. Grow this arb in full sun or light shade, and shelter it from strong winds to prevent browning. Provide a bit of TLC during hot, dry weather with deep and regular watering.
**Why we love it:** Birds appreciate the dense cover, and the brightly colored form will blow you away.

---

**TRUE DWARFS** *Before purchasing any small plant, be sure its mature size is what you need and want. According to the American Conifer Society, dwarf varieties can grow 1 to 6 inches per year, but make sure to check the tags on your specific variety for growth and mature size.*

---

adds year-round fiery color

### 8 Fire Chief globe arborvitae

*THUJA OCCIDENTALIS* 'CONGABE', ZONES 5 TO 8
SIZE: 3 TO 5 FEET TALL AND 3 TO 4 FEET WIDE

Add a touch of red and gold to your evergreen collection. As the seasons change, so does this conifer: You'll see new spring growth in bright gold, then deep red tips in fall. This perfectly shaped globe fits nicely in a rock garden, stands alone in a container or plays nice in a hedgerow. Grow it in full sun or partial shade.
**Why we love it:** No pruning is needed to keep up the round form.

extremely
adaptable pine

9

## 9 Dwarf scotch pine

*PINUS SYLVESTRIS* 'GLAUCA NANA',
ZONES 3 TO 7

SIZE: 5 TO 8 FEET TALL AND WIDE

Strong winds are no match for this rugged beauty. It adapts to a variety of soils and tolerates urban conditions, but it does struggle a bit in the summer heat of the South. Enjoy the peeling orange bark that contrasts nicely with the bluish-green needles.

**Why we love it:** This chameleon-like tree works well in Japanese and woodland gardens, either as a lone specimen or near a dry streambed or boulder.

10

## 10 Moon Frost hemlock

*TSUGA CANADENSIS* 'MOON FROST',
ZONES 4 TO 7

SIZE: 2 TO 4 FEET TALL AND 2 TO 4 FEET WIDE

Hemlocks are made for shade, and Moon Frost is no exception. Needles emerge white in spring for a frosty glow; in winter, look for a blush of pink. Grow in a cool location with partial to full shade and moist soil.

**Why we love it:** Hemlock's graceful look is lovely to incorporate throughout the landscape.

# Glad You Asked!

*Our pros tackle tricky blooming issues, caring for plants during the winter and more.*

**Q** I love peonies and have bought several types in the past years, but they have no smell. The best part of peonies is their fragrance. How can I get them to smell as good as they're supposed to?

**Linda Caldwell** NEWPORT, VIRGINIA

**MELINDA:** Fragrance varies from one variety of peony to the next. When selecting peonies, look for varieties that are advertised as fragrant. The red-flecked white flowers of the Festiva Maxima are considered one of the most aromatic. Flying Swallow in a Red Dress (an early bloomer) and Red Magic both have spicy fragrances. Snow Lotus' single flowers and the double-pink blossoms of Eden's Perfume also have an intense scent.

**Q** I planted a Honeygold and a Cortland apple tree about 4 years ago and have only had one apple. I noticed that the trees do not bloom at the same time. Should I plant a third apple tree in order to pollinate all three? If so, what type would be best? **Marge Berger** ATHENS, WISCONSIN

**MELINDA:** Age, growing conditions and plant health can influence when apples flower and produce fruit. Dwarf trees typically start flowering and fruiting two to four years after transplanting. Taller standard trees need more time to establish and typically do not start fruiting for five to seven years. Honeygold and Cortland are both midseason bloomers and listed as good pollinators for each other. The difference in the individual plants' health and growing conditions may be causing the difference in the bloom time. Add another midseason bloomer, such as McIntosh, Jonathan, Liberty or Empire, and it may help bridge the bloom time and increase pollination and fruit production.

**Q** The leaves on my wild cherry trees are growing smaller leaves right from their surfaces. What is going on?

**Sybil Collins** HEMINGWAY, SOUTH CAROLINA

**MELINDA:** Bizarre growths, called galls, can be found on cherries, maples, oaks, hackberries and many other plants. The growths are actually part of the plant. As certain insects such as mites, aphids and adelgids feed, the plant responds by forming growths around the actual insect. These types of galls are not harmful and no treatment is needed. In fact, when you notice the problem, the insect is usually tucked safely inside the growth.

**Q** We lost some bushes a few years ago because we had a dry, cold winter. I was told we should have watered. When and what plants should you water in the winter?

**Rebecca Williamson** BUSHNELL, ILLINOIS

**MELINDA:** It's true that many plants die from dehydration as well as cold winter temperatures. Continue to water trees, shrubs and perennials as needed as the weather cools. Water all of your plants thoroughly before the ground freezes. Another way to give plants a boost and help them survive is with mulch. Cover the soil with organic materials, such as twice-shredded bark, evergreen needles or shredded leaves. Mulch conserves moisture and moderates soil temperatures. All plants benefit from such care, but new plantings, borderline hardy specimens and evergreens should be your first priority because they are most susceptible to winter damage.

**Q** My 6-year-old vining hydrangea has never bloomed. It's 15 feet tall and spread out over a trellis. How can I encourage blooming?

**Alyssa Kadyk** SARVER, PENNSYLVANIA

**MELINDA:** You're definitely not alone. This is a common issue among gardeners who grow climbing hydrangeas. As you discovered, these plants take a long time to establish and start flowering. Avoid high-nitrogen, fast-release fertilizers that encourage leaf and stem growth but discourage flowering. Water plants thoroughly as needed and use a low-nitrogen, slow-release fertilizer if you feel your plants need a boost. Your patience will be rewarded with beautiful blooms.

Brown-eyed Susans
PHOTO BY VERONICA MCAVOY

Himalayan blue poppy
Finalist in our Backyard Photo Contest
**PHOTO BY BERNADETTE SEIFERT**

Holy Gate echeveria
Finalist in our Backyard Photo Contest
**PHOTO BY MIKE DROPPLEMAN**

Hesperoyucca
Finalist in our Backyard Photo Contest
**PHOTO BY DEBORAH SALDANA**

# CHAPTER 6

# Travel

Hop in the car because it's time for a road trip! We'll point you to the very best spots for birding adventures across the country. Whether you're in the mood for a guided tour, festival or independent journey, check here for your itinerary.

JOHANN SCHUMACHER DESIGN

# *FLORIDA* *BIRDING* *from the* *BYWAYS*

**An American avocet in winter plumage wades in shallow water.**

Look for vulturelike crested caracaras at Viera Wetlands.

*Whether you're a snowbird in for the season or vacationing for a week, find time to see the Sunshine State's best birds from the comfort of your car. Grab your family and your binoculars, buckle up, and take a cruise through these drivable hot spots.*

**BY JILL STAAKE**

## BLACK POINT WILDLIFE DRIVE
*Titusville*

When your Kennedy Space Center visit is complete, take a joyride through Merritt Island National Wildlife Refuge, which surrounds the high-tech complex. Seven-mile Black Point Wildlife Drive is one of the best places in Florida to see overwintering waterfowl.

*Watch For:* The variety of ducks in winter is a must-see! American coots gather by the thousands, along with northern pintails, American wigeons, blue-winged and green-winged teals, hooded mergansers, northern shovelers, redheads, and ring-necked ducks. Look overhead for raptors such as peregrine falcons and northern harriers. American avocets and long-billed dowitchers haunt the shallows at low tide.

*Nearby:* You're almost guaranteed to encounter the endemic Florida scrub-jay during an easy walk at the Helen and Allan Cruickshank Sanctuary. Drive or hike along the embankments at Viera Wetlands to see unique birds such as the crested caracara.

American white pelicans feeding at Merritt Island National Wildlife Refuge

Wind blows a reddish egret's wispy feathers.

### 10 FLORIDA BIRDS FOR YOUR LIFE LIST

| | |
|---|---|
| Roseate spoonbill | Crested caracara |
| Snail kite | Painted bunting |
| Black skimmer | American avocet |
| Limpkin | Reddish egret |
| Florida scrub-jay | Purple gallinule |

## J.N. "DING" DARLING NATIONAL WILDLIFE REFUGE WILDLIFE DRIVE

### *Sanibel Island*

Located near Fort Myers, Sanibel Island is a top vacation spot for those who love shelling and beachcombing. It's also home to J.N. "Ding" Darling National Wildlife Refuge, named for the conservationist who designed the first Federal Duck Stamp. A 4-mile route through mangrove-lined estuaries features multiple overlooks and an observation tower. Plan to visit several times throughout the day, as species vary based on tide levels.

*Watch For:* Roseate spoonbills spend low tide sweeping the shallows for food with their wide bills. White pelicans overwinter here in large numbers, and reddish egrets dash through shallow water in pursuit of prey. Watch black skimmers fly with open bills as they fish along the surface, and peer into waterside vegetation to find yellow-crowned night-herons.

*Nearby:* Keep your eyes peeled at Corkscrew Swamp Sanctuary for the fabulous rainbow-colored painted bunting. The sanctuary is also home to barred owls and other swampland birds.

This tricolored heron shows off its bill, bright blue in breeding season.

Painted bunting

American kestrel

## SHARK VALLEY TRAM TOUR
*Miami*

Ditch your car and hop on the tram for a two-hour trip in Everglades National Park, with a midway stop at an observation tower. Be prepared to see nearly every wading bird found in Florida. Your guide will help you identify them and tell you about efforts to control invasive predators, including the Burmese python, that threaten native wildlife.

*Watch For:* Great egrets, little blue herons, snowy egrets and tricolored herons are abundant. Snail kites soar overhead, along with ospreys and American kestrels. Smaller songbirds are here, too, including common yellowthroat warblers and loggerhead shrikes.

*Nearby:* The Anhinga Trail provides an opportunity to see plenty of its namesake anhingas and dozens of other wading species. Stroll the boardwalk to admire native bromeliads among the vegetation.

An osprey flies
with its latest catch.

## LAKE APOPKA WILDLIFE DRIVE
*Apopka*

Take a break from the theme parks in nearby Orlando and take a spin through 11 miles of reclaimed marshlands on the north shore of one of Florida's largest lakes. Once one of the state's most polluted areas due to farmland runoff, this area is now home to more than 250 bird species. Stream the free guided audio tour on your mobile device to learn about the restoration projects and local wildlife as you drive.

*Watch For:* Winter is the best time to look for least bitterns, which are easier to spot when there are fewer leaves on the vegetation. Resident black-bellied whistling-ducks are a cinch to find once you hear their high-pitched call. Fulvous whistling-ducks are sometimes found here, too.

*Nearby:* Walk the trails along the water reclamation ponds at Orlando Wetlands Park to discover both common and purple gallinules, or take the free tram ride on Fridays and Saturdays. Or head to Circle B Bar Reserve in nearby Lakeland to see bald eagles and wintering songbirds.

A large flock of
black skimmers

Anhinga in a mangrove tree at Ding Darling

Black-bellied whistling-duck

A great blue heron poses during sunrise at Viera Wetlands.

# where WOODS

Unlike other eastern warblers, prothonotary warblers nest in tree holes instead of out in the open.

# meet WATER

*From colorful warblers to elegant storks, unexpected beauty is all around you when you step into a swamp.* **BY KEN KEFFER**

**B**anish thoughts of deep shadows, dark water and lurking creatures. There's a lot more to swamps than you might think. Found in flood plains along streams and rivers, swamps provide flood control and natural filtration to keep local ecosystems healthy. Not to mention, plenty of birds and other animals live and thrive in these haunts.

But even the most celebrated swamps have identity issues. The Great Dismal Swamp, for example, is a name that may not entice visitors, but Deloras Freeman, the visitor services manager, says many folks enjoy the national wildlife refuge in Virginia and North Carolina. "The birders start showing up about a week before the warblers do in the spring," she says.

If the thought of wading through standing water doesn't appeal to you, many parks and refuges offer boardwalks so you can experience the swamps and keep your feet dry. And once you explore a swamp, you'll be rewarded with some of nature's most stunning critters, especially birds uniquely suited for this habitat of woods and water.

A wood stork's wingspan is over 5 feet long.

Although this white ibis is standing alone, these birds are very sociable and nest within large colonies.

## WADING BIRDS

Forget about walking along the boardwalk planks. Wading birds don't need 'em. Their long legs work just fine and are perfect for stalking fish in the backwaters. Although the waters are stained the color of tea, they aren't muddy or murky, which means that fish-eating birds can easily spot and scoop up a meal in the currents that flow slowly here.

Wood storks are the pickiest of the stand-and-wait crew. They need the water to be just right: not too deep or shallow. Audubon's Corkscrew Swamp Sanctuary in southern Florida hosts nesting pairs of wood storks in late winter when conditions are driest and the fish most concentrated.

Along the coastal southeastern states, white ibis forage among the cypress and mangrove trees. Unlike their name, young white ibises are mostly brown, but the adults are white as cotton. Similar in size and color to snowy egrets and immature little blue herons, white ibises are recognized by their reddish pink bills and legs. They use their down-curved bills to probe for invertebrates in the mud or catch insects.

Hairy woodpecker

## WOODPECKERS

Although the vast expanses of flooded timberlands in the Southeast remain mysterious and underexplored, few people hold out hope that the presumably extinct ivory-billed woodpecker survives there. But, only slightly smaller than the ivory-billed, pileated woodpeckers do inhabit the swamps, along with the more familiar woodpecker species like downy, hairy and red-bellied.

Historically, the wet nature of swamps made logging efforts extremely difficult. Areas that weren't diked, drained and harvested now hold some of the largest trees. Nearly the size of crows, pileated woodpeckers require big trees for their rectangular-shaped nest cavities, so they're naturally drawn to setting up shop in swampy areas.

## WARBLERS

Woodpeckers are known for hammering out holes, but once they leave their homemade tree houses behind, sunny warblers with blue wings take up residence in the woodpeckers' excavated apartments. As well as in tree cavities, these stunning prothonotary warblers nest in bird boxes. "Prothonotary warblers nest in areas where people can see them," says Deloras. Found in eastern swamps from central Florida to southern Minnesota, they use boxes placed 4 to 12 feet high that look out over the water.

The Great Dismal Swamp has less standing water than other places like Okefenokee or the Everglades. Instead, the seasonally flooded woodland provides a forest floor where Swainson's warblers are seen skulking along. "The thick deciduous forest can make it hard to see the birds in summer," Deloras says. But birding by ear alone can be especially rewarding, she says, and spring and fall migration brings an explosion of bird activity to these strange but lively habitats.

This female pileated woodpecker may have helped hollow out the nest cavity, but the male did the heavy lifting.

Two wood storks perch on a tree limb overlooking Lake Corpus Christi in Texas.

## SEE A SWAMP

*Canoes and kayak trails are available in some locations, and hikes through swamps also are possible, thanks to boardwalks, trails and dikes.*

- Audubon's Corkscrew Swamp Sanctuary, Florida

- Okefenokee National Wildlife Refuge, Georgia and Florida

- Congaree National Park, South Carolina

- Great Dismal Swamp National Wildlife Refuge, Virginia and North Carolina

- Blackwater National Wildlife Refuge, Maryland

- Great Swamp National Wildlife Refuge, New Jersey

# The Best of Ohio Birding

*Go "where the birds are" when you visit the shores of Lake Erie.* **JUDY ROBERTS**

*Warbler Capital of the World*

**OHIO**

**FIELD EDITOR**

## WHY I LOVE IT

Birders from around the world flock to Magee Marsh and other northwest Ohio hot spots. A prime time is spring, when migrating warblers and other birds choose the shores of Lake Erie as their stopping-over point on their long journey northward.

## THE BIGGEST WEEK

Whether you're a newbie or a seasoned birder, the area (known as the Warbler Capital of the World) is a must-visit, especially during The Biggest Week in American Birding (*bwiab.com*), a festival organized by the Black Swamp Bird Observatory that coincides with spring migration. The boardwalk at Magee Marsh, near Oak Harbor, runs through a patch of woods where more

than 30 warbler species, including cerulean and blackpoll, flit through the trees. Follow the Biggest Week account on Twitter (*@biggestweek*) to be notified when rare and exciting birds appear. And stop by the Ottawa National Wildlife Refuge to see species like dunlins and eastern kingbirds.

## DIG IN

Gardeners should check out Bench Farms, a great greenhouse near Curtice that sells plants to attract birds and butterflies. (Look for the "welcome birders" sign.) If you love

flowers but prefer to keep your hands out of the dirt, tour Schedel Arboretum & Gardens, a 17-acre paradise in Elmore with Japanese, rose, peony and other gardens.

## ESSENTIALS

**EAT** Homemade pie at Blackberry Corner Tavern in Martin

**STAY** Maumee Bay State Park Lodge in Oregon— it's also the conference headquarters for The Biggest Week

**PLAY** Cheer on the Toledo Mud Hens, a minor league baseball team, at Fifth Third Field, Toledo

Crowds of excited birders gather on the boardwalk at Magee Marsh to see flocks of colorful migrating warblers, like the Kirtland's (above) and the Magnolia (below).

**TRIVIA** *The rare Kirtland's warbler has been spotted here. Your best chance to see it this year is at The Biggest Week in American Birding, starting the first Friday in May.*

# The City of Roses

*From food pods to an extinct volcano, this area has plenty of quirky qualities to discover.*

**MARY ANNE THYGESEN** PORTLAND, OREGON

Portland

OREGON

FIELD EDITOR

## WHY I LOVE IT

Portland is a foodie's paradise, but what makes this city unique is its staggering number of food carts. Over 500 of the carts are found in groups called "pods" throughout the city, and there's a delicious dish for everyone, whether you love doughnuts or fresh fish tacos.

## SPOT THE SWIFTS

Mount Tabor Park, a huge park on top of an extinct volcano, is a must for visiting birders. Species such as white-crowned sparrows, Wilson's warblers and willow flycatchers have been spotted here. If you're in Portland in the fall, make sure you see the thousands of migrating Vaux's swifts that pass through the city

on their way to Central and South America. Their most popular perch is the Chapman School smokestack, and onlookers watch as the birds swoop and soar around it before resting inside for the night.

## SEE SPECTACULAR FALL COLORS

The Portland Japanese Garden is a can't-miss hot spot, no matter what season it is, but fall is a particularly good time to go. The garden bursts into gorgeous fiery reds, thanks to the many Japanese maples there. The garden

is 5.5 acres including an authentic teahouse and hosts events, like an October moon-viewing festival called O-Tsukimi. A few other parks and gardens to check out while you're here include the Portland International Rose Test Garden, Lan Su Chinese Garden and Silver Falls State Park.

## ESSENTIALS

**EAT** The food cart pod Tidbit Food Farm and Garden
**STAY** Benson Hotel; it's pet-friendly
**PLAY** Portland Thorns women's soccer game at Providence Park

**Visit the Portland Japanese Garden (top) for the tranquil scenery. Then, head to Mount Tabor Park to see bird species like the Wilson's warbler (above).**

**TRIVIA** *Powell's City of Books is Portland's giant indie bookstore, with over 3,500 different sections to browse, including a rare book room.*

# Say Hello to Salina

*Discover a small Kansas gem nestled in the center of the state.* **BOBBY HIEBERT JR.** SALINA, KANSAS

✗ *Salina*
**KANSAS**

**FIELD EDITOR**

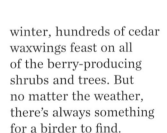

## WHY I LOVE IT
There's always something to see and do in Salina, whether it's catching a musical performance at the art deco Stiefel Theatre, which opened in 1931, or stopping by Smoky Hill Museum, a small, Kansas-centric free museum about the history of the heartland.

## 365 DAYS OF BIRDS
Lakewood Park should be the first stop in Salina for any visiting birder. Thanks to its habitat mix of prairie, woodland and lake, a wide range of species exists here. Wood ducks float across the water, colorful migrating warblers pass through in spring and blue-gray gnatcatchers are here to nest. In summer, be on the lookout for roosting Mississippi kites. In winter, hundreds of cedar waxwings feast on all of the berry-producing shrubs and trees. But no matter the weather, there's always something for a birder to find.

## GO BOULDERING
Just south of Lakewood Park is Indian Rock Park, which has easy-to-follow hiking trails and offers nature brochures so visitors can identify the 100 species of wildflowers growing along the routes. If you're itching for a little adventure and have some bouldering experience, try climbing across the overhung boulder located just off the trail.

## ESSENTIALS
**EAT** Tiny, onion-laden sliders sold by the sack at The Cozy Inn
**STAY** Locally owned bed and breakfast, The End Iron Inn, also housed the Salina Telephone Company in 1905
**PLAY** Treat yourself to a show at the Salina Community Theatre

**Wood duck pairs (top), blue-gray gnatcatchers (middle) and Mississippi kites (below) are a few of Lakewood Park's most sought-after bird species.**

**TRIVIA** *The title character of* Thoroughly Modern Millie *leaves Salina for the Big Apple, where she hopes to marry a rich businessman. The original 1967 film starred Julie Andrews and Mary Tyler Moore.*

# Find the
# PERFECT
# *Festival*

*From tiny hummingbirds in Arizona to elegant hawks in New Jersey, there's a bird party out there for everyone.*

**BY KAITLIN STAINBROOK**

Swarms of birders (left) gather when rare birds such as this Kirtland's warbler are spotted at the Biggest Week in American Birding festival in Ohio.

The first bird festival I ever attended was possibly the largest one in the United States: the Biggest Week in American Birding. And I'll admit, the only image I could picture beforehand was hundreds of super serious birders wearing khaki vests. But once there, looking around at all the other festivalgoers, I realized the crowd wasn't exactly as I'd imagined. I saw a lot of beginning birders, from 10-year-olds with binoculars dangling from their necks to excited retirees eagerly flipping through field guides. Whether they were first-timers like me or Biggest Week veterans, birders of all skill levels gathered together with their birding gear, enthusiastically bonding over a Blackburnian warbler flitting from branch to branch nearby.

Besides talks, presentations and abundant birding, the Sedona Hummingbird Festival has fantastic views, like this one of Cathedral Rock.

It turns out, there's no typical birder, because birding is for everyone. And there's no better way to experience that joy than by going to a bird festival. Pick the one that's right for you and join one of the most passionate and welcoming communities around.

## FOR THE NEWBIE
### Biggest Week in American Birding
### Oak Harbor, Ohio

As soon as you step onto the Magee Marsh boardwalk, you'll realize why this 10-day May festival is called Biggest Week. Thousands of birders flock to this town to see the roughly 36 warbler species that visit during spring migration and a dazzling variety of other birds. The rare Kirtland's warbler has been known to pass through the area and was spotted last year. (It's difficult for most birders to find because it nests only in Michigan's jack pines.)

The festival, organized by Black Swamp Bird Observatory, is an ideal choice for beginning birders new to the scene, because most of the birding is fairly easy. Many of the warblers are at or near eye level, and waterbirds stay at close range. Plus, plenty of enthusiastic guides and experts are stationed on the boardwalk, ready to help spot and point out colorful warblers as well as answer questions. Head to *bsbo.org* for more information.

## FOR THE HUMMINGBIRD FAN
### Sedona Hummingbird Festival
### Sedona, Arizona

If you want to get close enough to hummingbirds that you can count their feathers or hear the magical hum of tiny wings beating so fast they're a blur, the Sedona Hummingbird Festival is the place for you. From presentations on conservation efforts to tips on capturing these sprightly little birds in a photo, experts deliver plenty of programming for every hummingbird enthusiast. "This isn't like any other festival you've been to before," says Ross Hawkins, founder of the nonprofit

See species like the calliope (above) and male Anna's (right) at the Sedona Hummingbird Festival. And don't miss bird-banding demos (below).

organization The Hummingbird Society. "And the friendships you make here, connecting with other hummingbird lovers, can last for decades."

Once your head is filled with enough hummingbird facts, you can tour private gardens specially designed to attract loads of species, like calliope, Anna's, rufous, broad-tailed and black-chinned. Or check out banding stations, where you can see these beautiful birds up close as licensed pros attach mini numbered bands to bird legs to track their movement with the Bird Banding Lab.

The festival is always held at

## BIRDER DECODER
*Fit in at your next festival when you use this lingo.*

**BIG YEAR:** a personal challenge or friendly competition to see how many bird species you can spot in a year

**BINS:** binoculars

**FIRST OF THE YEAR (FOY):** the first of a species seen that year

**LIFE LIST:** a running list birders keep of every species they've seen in their lifetime

**NEMESIS BIRD:** a species that continuously eludes a birder trying to spot it

**PISH:** the call a birder makes to lure a songbird closer

**SPARK BIRD:** the species that kicks off someone's lifelong birding passion

**SOB:** spouse of a birder

Cape May Fall Festival attendees (below) observe and count raptor species, like this peregrine falcon.

peak hummingbird time, either the last weekend of July or the first weekend of August. (In 2017 the festival dates were July 28-30.) If you're sweating the idea of visiting Arizona in high summer, you'll be in for a cool surprise: Sedona is in the mountains, so it's less sweltering than the rest of Arizona. Ross says, "The festival tagline is 'the most beautiful place in America to see hummingbirds,' and that's no exaggeration." Check out *hummingbirdsociety.org* to learn more about the festival.

## FOR THE MIGRATION MANIAC

### Cape May Fall Festival
### Cape May, New Jersey

Get your binoculars ready and look up! Cape May is a superhighway for migrating birds, especially in October, when thousands of hawk species—like American kestrels, peregrine falcons, merlins, Cooper's and sharp-shinneds—travel to their southern hunting grounds. Visit the cape during the Cape May Fall Festival near the end of October. Last year's festival offered guided walks for beginners and advanced

birders, an overnight pelagic trip, and a convention hall open to the public and packed with vendors.

Many other birds join the raptors in the Cape May skies, though. Migrating songbirds such as blackpolls, red-eyed vireos, and yellow-rumped and palm warblers make the trip, too. (Here's a secret: Go to Higbee Beach at dawn and you may witness tens of thousands of migrating songbirds bursting into the sky.) The tally at the end of the festival usually edges up to 200 species seen in total. Go online at *njaudubon.org*.

Head to the Harlingen, Texas, bird festival to see uncommon birds like green jays, which can be seen only at this particular spot without crossing the U.S.-Mexico border.

## PACKING CHECKLIST
*Grab your favorite suitcase and get geared up for a great birding adventure!*

- ○ Backpack
- ○ Binoculars
- ○ Camera
- ○ Field guide
- ○ Gloves or hand warmers
- ○ Lightweight hiking boots
- ○ Rain jacket
- ○ Warm layers of clothing
- ○ Water bottle
- ○ Weatherproof notebook

## FOR THE LIFE LISTER
**Rio Grande Valley Birding Festival Harlingen, Texas**

There's nothing like a well-organized life list, the ongoing tally of different bird species a birder has ever seen. But as you spot more and more species, it becomes harder to find new-to-you birds. The Rio Grande Valley Birding Festival is the perfect place to beef up your list. The valley sits close to Mexico, so birds uncommon in the U.S., like green jays and great kiskadees, often move back and forth across the border here.

Birders at all skill levels are welcome here, and the festival, usually held in early November, is particularly known for having small guided tours led by experts in the field. If you prefer a fast pace, check out some of the "big day" tours, where festivalgoers ride in separate vans along different routes to see who can spot the most bird species. Visit the festival's official website at *rgvbf.org* and keep your life list growing!

# CHAPTER 7

# Homegrown Harvest

Take your vegetable plot from good to great with these handy harvest tips. Discover creative solutions for small-space gardening, successful techniques for growing a top-shelf tomato and other edibles, and easy ideas to stretch your summer crop into fall.

SAXON HOLT

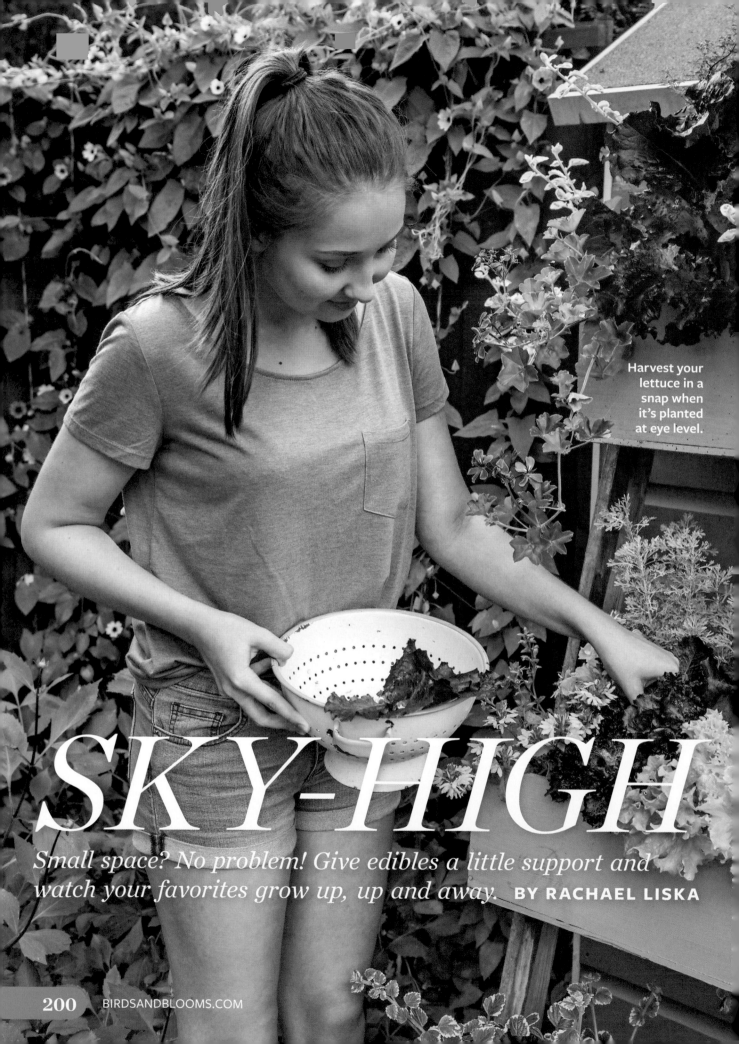

Harvest your lettuce in a snap when it's planted at eye level.

# SKY-HIGH

*Small space? No problem! Give edibles a little support and watch your favorites grow up, up and away.* **BY RACHAEL LISKA**

Let scarlet runner beans climb with the aid of a teepee.

# VEGGIES

*t*hings are looking up for those who crave farm-fresh veggies but have little to no acreage. A vertical vegetable garden is the ultimate solution for your small-space backyard. It's easy to do, and your favorite veggies—tomatoes, green beans and cucumbers, to name a few—are *up* for the job.

Container-grown or vertical veggies are perfect for condo or apartment dwellers, or anyone who deals with difficult terrain or soil conditions. That's because vertical gardens can be placed almost anywhere—a balcony, patio, front porch or along a fence. And you can grow more veggies per square foot this way than in a more traditional garden. Plus harvesting is a breeze with the fruits of your labor right in front of you. No more stooping!

Vertical options also offer people living in close confines a little privacy. A partition covered in edible greenery works wonders to separate you from prying neighbors. The same goes for eyesores like air-conditioning units and compost bins. Hide them from view with a screen of green beans or a teepee of tomatoes.

As you start planning the vertical garden of your dreams, keep these tips in mind.

• For the best yield, find a location that enjoys full sun and is sheltered from high winds.

• If planting on a balcony, consider anchoring or weighing your vertical structures down so they won't be able to topple over during inclement weather.

• Plant along the north side of your garden bed so you don't cast shade on other plants.

• Anything not directly planted into the ground dries out quicker. Check the soil moisture of your raised beds and containers regularly, especially in warmer months. Make frequent watering easier by planting near a water source, whether it's a spot your hose reaches or a place where you can carry a watering can.

## CREATIVE CONTAINERS AND STRUCTURES

From lattice panels to ladders, almost anything can be used or repurposed to reap a bounty of fresh rewards.

"Vertical garden containers are limitless," says Chris McLaughlin, author of *Vertical Vegetable Gardening*. "Use anything you find that holds soil and has drainage. Supports for climbing plants can be woven fencing, ladders, gates, chicken wire, netting or trellises."

Shelves are also an excellent way to support an array of containers packed with anything from parsley to potatoes. Keep in mind that a little elbow room goes a long way in terms of adequate air circulation.

If you're a renter, some thing a little less permanent may be more appealing. Perch and anchor containers on the steps of a ladder, or fix chicken wire or a repurposed

shutter to a wall and hang pots of produce from it. Stack some growing boxes or even cinder blocks to create a base for a living wall.

Maybe you already have a raised garden bed but want to try your hand at growing up. Consider using tall, slender structures like bamboo poles, teepees and tomato cages, or even make-a-statement architectural elements like arbors, trellises and fencing.

"One of my favorite vertical designs is a cattle panel 'arch' that connects one raised garden bed to another," Chris says. "T-posts support the panels, and climbing plants at each end are trained to grow overhead. This is a great way to take advantage of the space lost between beds, while still maintaining a viable walkway. The hanging produce offers visual appeal and is easy to harvest."

Vining and trailing crops that

Grow vining veggies, like peas, on a wicker trellis for support.

An A-frame trellis helps to maximize space in small backyards.

can be coaxed to climb or grow gracefully toward the ground are best bets when it comes to selecting the right produce for your plot. Most can be secured to supports with ties and clips.

However, some heavier edibles, like melons, may need slings to keep them from slipping off the vine. That's when old pantyhose really come in handy! Simply use them or other bits of scrap material to make hammocks that you can attach to the support.

Yet another good use of space is to plant salad greens, such as spinach, arugula and lettuce, at the foot of your vertical vegetable garden. Leafy greens generally tolerate more shade from the plants suspended above, and the cooler surroundings may actually allow you to grow them well into the hot summer months. Talk about a bonus!

## TOP 10 VERTICALS
*Raise the roof with these edible contenders.*

1. Pole beans
2. Sugar snap and snow peas (vining varieties)
3. Squash (summer and dwarf winter varieties)
4. Tomatoes (vining varieties)
5. Melons like cantaloupes or mini watermelons
6. Cucumbers (vining varieties)
7. Climbing spinach
8. Grapes
9. Climbing nasturtiums (both leaves and flowers are edible)
10. Kiwi

Raspberries

Berries just got better thanks to new dwarf varieties suited for smaller spaces. A tinier plant means these delightful gems live right at home inside your favorite patio pot. The next time you crave a handful of fresh berries for your bowl of cereal or a smoothie, all you'll have to do is step outside your door.

## BLACKBERRIES

Choose a thornless variety and plant it in a wide, shallow container. The long canes need to be tied, so insert a few strong stakes or place the pot next to a trellis to keep the plant growing straight and upright. If you are not sure where to start, try Baby Cakes, which is 3 to 4 feet tall and thornless, with bright, white flowers in spring and large, zingy blackberries in summer. In some regions, it offers another crop of sweetness in midautumn.

Blackberries

# Sweeten Up Your Pots

*Add pops of color to your patio with berry plants that fit neatly inside containers.*

BY CRYSTAL RENNICKE

Strawberries

## POWER UP YOUR POTS

*Become a potting pro and give your berries the TLC they need.*

**PLANT:** For most berries, choose 5-gallon pots that are 24 inches wide and offer plenty of drainage. Berries need 6 to 8 hours of full sun.

**PICK:** Harvest your yummy blueberries and strawberries when they break off the stems, your raspberries when they slip off the receptacle.

**PRUNE:** After harvesting, remove any fruited stems by cutting them at the base. Pruning varies depending on the type of plant, so research first!

Blackberries

Blueberries

## BLUEBERRIES

Use a potting mix with acidic soil and fertilize in early and late spring to promote growth and fruit production. Peach Sorbet is a self-pollinating plant with a rainbow of leaves ranging from peachy pink to emerald green. Another tantalizing blueberry option is Jelly Bean. It produces a crop of super-sweet berries in midsummer.

## RASPBERRIES

Look for fall-bearing dwarf raspberry varieties. Apply a generous amount of compost and balanced fertilizer in early and late spring. For a thorn-free raspberry plant with a compact growth habit, look no further than Raspberry Shortcake. It grows best in full sun and in soil with good drainage.

## STRAWBERRIES

Everbearing varieties work best for containers. Pick a pot or hanging basket at least 18 inches wide and 8 inches deep. Give Quinault a go when you're ready to plant. It's everbearing and produces heavy fruits. Try other varieties like Tribute or Seascape. Delizz, a 2016 All-America Selections winner, is a good choice, too, because it grows fast from seed to harvest.

### STUFF WE LOVE

Get your berry fix at *bushelandberry.com*, a one-stop shop for all your mini berry plant needs, including most of the varieties mentioned on the pages here.

# Quick-to-Grow Veggies

*Plant these crops for your fastest summer harvest ever.*  BY NIKI JABBOUR

**TURN UP THE SWEET**
These super veggies are loaded with iron, calcium and vitamin C. Turnips also tolerate fall frosts and become sweeter in cool weather.

1

### 1 Hakurei turnip
*BRASSICA RAPA*
38 DAYS TO HARVEST

Quick-growing salad turnips, like Hakurei, are popular at farmers markets but are easy to grow at home, too. Ready to dig up just weeks after seeding, they are known as a dual-purpose crop, yielding sweet roots as well as tasty greens for salads and stir-fries. **Why we love it:** The golf ball-size roots are delicious raw, cooked or pickled.

### 2 Smooth-leaf spinach
*SPINACIA OLERACEA*
38 DAYS TO HARVEST

Seed companies offer three types of spinach: savoy, semi-savoy and smooth-leaf. For rapid growth, stick with smooth varieties like Corvair or Space. Their round-to-oval leaves stay compact and maintain their quality for an extended harvest season. **Why we love it:** Long stems and flat foliage make harvesting and washing a snap.

### 3 Adelaide carrot
*DAUCUS CAROTA* VAR. *SATIVUS*
50 DAYS TO HARVEST

Forget the imposter baby carrots found in the supermarket. Adelaide is a true baby carrot, with 3- to 4-inch-long roots and a mild flavor. It's also among the earliest carrots to mature, with roots that are ready to be pulled in just seven weeks. **Why we love it:** Even those without gardens can grow these baby carrots by sowing seeds in pots or window boxes.

---

**RADISHES ANY WHICH WAY** *Generally speaking, the longer you allow radishes to grow, the spicier they will taste when you dig them up. Let 'em linger, but not too long—otherwise they become pithy rather than more flavorful.*

---

### 4 Cherry Belle radish
*RAPHANUS SATIVUS*
22 DAYS TO HARVEST

For over 60 years, this award-winning variety has been a garden standard, and for good reason. It offers an extra-early harvest of small, rounded roots with cherry red skin and crisp white flesh. This crop can be harvested three weeks after seeding. **Why we love it:** Radishes are edible from top to bottom! Eat the roots and leaves, then let a few plants flower for the blooms and crunchy seed pods.

### 5 Tatsoi
*BRASSICA RAPA*
VAR. *NARINOSA*
45 DAYS TO HARVEST

Tatsoi is a quick-growing mustard that forms low rosettes of spoon-shaped, deep green leaves. It has a mild flavor and can be eaten raw or cooked. Tatsoi is very hardy, thriving in fall gardens and winter cold frames. **Why we love it:** Light-challenged gardeners appreciate that tatsoi plants grow well even in partial shade.

### 6 Kale
*BRASSICA OLERACEA*
65 DAYS TO HARVEST

This superfood not only packs a nutritional punch but is speedy from seed to harvest, too. Among the quickest to grow are smooth-leaved varieties like Toscano and Red Russian, which can be harvested as greens a mere month from sowing. **Why we love it:** The leaves of recently sprouted kale are more tender than those harvested from mature plants.

### 7 Tokyo Bekana cabbage
*BRASSICA RAPA* VAR. *PEKINENSIS*
30 DAYS TO HARVEST

Although Tokyo Bekana looks like lettuce, it's actually a loose-leaf type of Chinese cabbage. Slender white stems hold attractive rosettes of crinkly lime-green leaves. The flavor is sweet and mild, and the plants tolerate cold, thriving in early spring and autumn. **Why we love it:** This easy-to-grow green is perfect for garden beds but works well in window boxes and containers, too.

---

**HOW TO HARVEST SNOWED-IN KALE** *Cooler temps prompt kale to turn stored starch into sugars, which makes it even sweeter. It's even OK to harvest after a snowfall! Give your yield a further boost by harvesting outer leaves when they're 8 to 10 inches tall.*

---

### 8 Arugula
*ERUCA SATIVA*
40 DAYS TO HARVEST

The peppery leaves of arugula have been adding zip to salads for more than 2,000 years, and for good reason. This gourmet green is super fast, with baby leaves ready just three weeks from seeding. After you've had your fill of greens, allow a few plants to flower. The dainty blooms are edible and add a pretty pop of color to salads. **Why we love it:** Arugula thrives in cool weather and can be planted as soon as the soil has thawed in early spring.

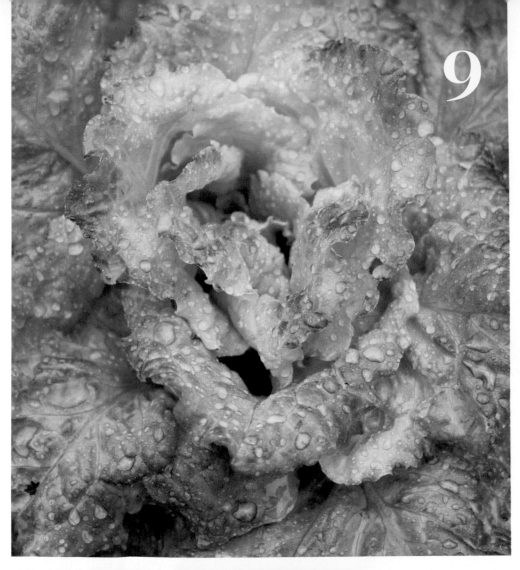

## 9 Leaf lettuce
*LACTUCA SATIVA*
45 DAYS TO HARVEST

There are many types of lettuce, but for sheer speed, you can't beat this one. Harvest-ready in six weeks, it comes in a variety of leaf colors and textures. Best bets include Red Salad Bowl, Black Seeded Simpson and Merlot. Start sowing the seeds in early spring, and plant more every few weeks for months of homegrown lettuce. **Why we love it:** Leaf lettuce is both pretty and productive. Tuck it into spring containers with pansies for an eye-catching, edible combination.

## 10 Petite Snap-Greens pea
*PISUM SATIVUM,* 30 DAYS TO HARVEST

If you love cute leafy greens, you'll want to give Petite Snap-Greens a whirl. It's a new variety grown for its dense clusters of edible leaflets, not for the pods or peas themselves. Sow seeds in pots or beds and begin harvesting the leafy tendrils soon after they form.

**Why we love it:** The pleasant crunch of the leaflets add bright flavor to pastas, salads, stir-fries and wraps.

---

### SNAP UP MORE SPEEDY VEGGIES
*Get growing in a jiffy with these veggie varieties, new in 2017.*

- **PATIO PRIDE PEA** Ready to harvest six weeks from seeding, this 2017 All-America Selections award-winner bears plump edible pods. It grows about a foot tall and is a fantastic find for hanging baskets.

- **PAYLOAD SQUASH** Disease resistance and heavy yields of smooth green fruits in 45 days make this summer squash a real winner.

- **KORIST KOHLRABI** Crisp, rounded stems of kohlrabi are delicious raw or cooked. Korist grows 4 inches wide. Begin harvesting 55 days after sowing seeds.

- **PORCH PICK BUSH BEAN** No space is no problem. Porch Pick forms compact plants for small gardens or containers. Expect a bumper crop of tender green pods 55 days from sowing.

Choose dwarf varieties, like this Bitonto F1 tomato bush, to grow in small containers.

# Grow a Terrific Tomato Crop

*Plant your most fruitful harvest ever with these seven tried-and-tested tips for success.*

Tomatoes are the bright red gems of veggie gardens. Up your grow game with these tomato tips from the National Garden Bureau.

## 1. LOOK FOR THE SUNNY SIDE

Set yourself up for success by making sure tomatoes are planted in a space that receives a lot of direct sunlight. "They can get by with six hours of sun but, ideally, eight hours or more is best," says Diane Blazek, executive director of the National Garden Bureau. "Less than eight hours of sunlight results in fewer and smaller fruits." Warm weather is important, too. Until nighttime temperatures reach 55 degrees, hold off on planting.

## 2. TRY THE TRENCH METHOD

Dig a 4-inch hole that's as long as the plant is high. Pluck lower leaves off the stem, then place the plant in the trench horizontally, filling the trench with soil but keeping the remaining leaves above the ground. "Planting horizontally in a trench or simply planting deeper in the soil allows the stem to shoot out new roots, giving the plant a sturdier base," Diane says. This method is ideal for large indeterminate tomatoes that develop heavy vines and fruits. The technique also promotes speedy, healthy growth, because the plant grows toward the sun and the developing roots are buried shallowly to stay warm. Just make sure to water deeply.

### 3. GIVE 'EM SHELTER

Tuck tomatoes in at night with a cloche or other cover to protect them from frosty temps. Diane suggests a cold frame (for seedlings), tunnel row covers (once plants are in the ground), water barriers, or an old cloth or plastic tarp. If exposed to 32 degrees, these plants will likely die, so shelter is key!

### 4. WATER WELL

As long as the plant continues to fruit, water deeply and thoroughly during dry periods. Once established, tomato plants need at least 1 inch of water a week.

### 5. SWIPE RIPE

Be patient and wait until tomatoes are fully ripened and at their deepest color before harvesting. (Once the fruit is removed, its sugar supply is cut off.) Gently twist the fruit so the stem separates easily from the vine.

### 6. SKIP THE REFRIGERATOR

Keep ripe tomatoes cozy instead of cool. Store at room temperature on a kitchen counter for a better-tasting bite. "Never store tomatoes in the fridge!" Diane says. "Refrigeration changes the taste and texture of tomatoes. Keep them at room temperature and use them as soon as they ripen."

### 7. GO GREEN

Before the first frost pays your garden a visit, pluck any remaining green tomatoes and place them on a windowsill or counter. If the tomato is in a warm spot, the fruit will ripen faster; a cooler location will slow ripening. Although the flavor won't match vine-ripened, it will stretch your harvest a little more.

### MEET THE NATIONAL GARDEN BUREAU

*This nonprofit has evolved since its Victory Garden efforts during World War II. Today, it educates and inspires green thumbs to grow their best gardens.*

### DEBUTS FRESH FROM THE VINE

- Oh Happy Day beefsteak hybrid is delicious on a burger or sandwich. The disease-resistant plants grow juicy 5-ounce fruits.

- Gladiator hybrid, a champion Roma, is a tangy addition to soups and salsas. Its 8-ounce fruits grow well in small spaces, like patios.

- Maglia Rosa Italian cherry tomatoes reach their peak flavor when the 3-inch-long fruits are light pink. Grow them in hanging baskets to pop one into your mouth whenever you like.

# GROW
## *a Veggie Sequel*

*Finish the season strong with these*
**5** *tips for the ultimate bonus harvest.*

**BY HEATHER LAMB**

Plant cool-weather vegetables, such as cabbage and chard, to have a second harvest in late summer.

A new season brings fresh opportunities to experiment in the garden, and fall is not an exception. After the height of summer, use a technique called succession planting to sow more vegetables and extend your growing season.

With succession planting, you are able to harvest another round of veggies before the winter frost. It's the perfect opportunity to try new varieties or make up for any spring procrastination that may have doomed leafy greens.

As a bonus, some vegetables are more flavorful when they mature in cooler seasons. "If you plant wisely and watch the calendar, you can get tastier vegetables in the fall for those that prefer cooler temperatures," says David Trinklein of the University of Missouri extension service.

Now is the ideal time to give your garden a second chance.

# 1 Know Your Growing Conditions

Start by figuring out the expected date of the first killing frost for your area. This is key to determining what and when to plant. The best place to find this information is the book farmers and gardeners have turned to since 1792: *The Old Farmer's Almanac*. You can find a copy in most grocery stores, but conveniently, its website (*almanac.com/weather*) has handy guides on both first frosts and planting dates for second-season crops.

# 2 Prepare the Garden

Weeds can be pesky challenges to late-summer gardening, because they've had all season to gain strong footholds. Weed meticulously and work fresh organic matter into the garden to provide a healthy start for fall veggies. This also improves soil that might have become depleted during summer.

# 3 Pick the Right Plants

Vegetables for late harvests fall into three categories, David says. First are the veggies that are intolerant of frost but that mature quickly, usually in 30 to 45 days. Second are those that take longer to mature but can withstand a little frost. Third, there are the long-maturing selections that tolerate some freezing temperatures.

In that first category are plants such as bush beans and many herbs, like basil. The second grouping contains a sweeping variety of vegetables, including broccoli, carrots, cilantro, collards, kale, peas and spinach. Many of these thrive even as temperatures dip into the 20s.

The third category contains garden selections that don't thrive in heat but are somewhat freeze-tolerant, such as Brussels sprouts and turnips. Cabbage and radishes also take to cold well, but mature fast.

# 4 Take Proper Care

Sowing seeds in late summer requires a few adjustments to your gardening routine. When planting seeds that prefer cooler temps to germinate, sow a little deeper in order to mimic a cool environment. For example, if you normally plant a seed at a depth of twice its diameter in spring, try planting at a depth

## LATE SEASON BLOOMS

While you're planting veggies, tuck in some cool-season annuals and perennials, too. Autumn stars such as flowering cabbage and chrysanthemums thrive through the first fall frost. Early spring blooms deserve a return engagement as well. Selections like pansies, dwarf snapdragons and violas perk up the early fall backyard.

Start Dazzling Blue kale in late summer for sweeter flavor.

An edible mixed garden bed can include herbs, vegetables and flowers.

of three to four times its diameter. Just be sure the soil is in good condition, so the sprout doesn't have to struggle to break through a layer of summer-hardened top crust. After a hot, dry season, it's sometimes difficult to tell how dry the subsoil is, so it's even more important to water the seeds and continue to do so regularly.

## 5 Be Patient

It's true that gardeners in northern regions may struggle to get anything but the fastest-growing, most frost-resistant varieties to grow from seed in time to harvest. Try radishes! They mature quickly and can be harvested until the soil freezes. Carrots and peas also are fine with light frost. To make the process easier, start longer-maturity varieties indoors, just as you would for spring transplanting. Southern gardeners, on the other hand, will likely see success with cool-season veggies well after the heat of summer has passed.

If you've picked the right frost-tolerant or fast-growing varieties for your area, you will reap a second (or third) harvest. Trust your plants and be patient. "You can't rush," David says. "The fact is it does take nature time to produce something that is worthwhile." And that's definitely worth waiting for.

## KEEP YOUR COOL

*Have a second harvest with these 13 veggie picks for fall weather.*

- **ARUGULA**
- **BOK CHOY**
- **BROCCOLI**
- **BUSH BEANS**
- **CABBAGE**
- **CARROTS**
- **CAULIFLOWER**
- **KALE**
- **LEAF LETTUCE**
- **RADISHES**
- **RUTABAGA**
- **SPINACH**
- **SWISS CHARD**

# Grow Veggies All Year Long

*For fresh salad fixings long into winter, shield your leafy greens from the elements.* **BY NIKI JABBOUR**

A cold frame with a clear top lets sunlight in.

A year-round veggie garden is possible! "By choosing the right plants, putting them in the ground at the right time, and providing some protection, anyone can extend the season," says Doug Oster, editor of the website Everybody Gardens. Try these techniques to keep your edibles growing longer.

## KEEP PLANTS COZY

Row covers are fabric blankets used to protect crops from frost. Lay them directly on top of plants or "floated" over garden beds. "I use 11-gauge wire from the hardware store to make low hoops to support the row cover," Doug says. "I've found keeping the hoops low, only a foot tall, gives the plants a better survival rate."

## BUILD A MINI GREENHOUSE

A mini hoop tunnel is like a small-scale greenhouse that shelters your crops in late fall into winter. The tunnels are easy to build—all you need is hoops and a cover. Make the hoops from lengths of ½-inch diameter PVC or metal conduit bent in a U-shape. To insulate your crops, cover the hoops with a plastic sheet and use clips to secure the plastic to the hoops.

Create a DIY hoop house with netting or plastic sheets.

## DOUG'S FAVORITE WINTER CROP

*Besides cold-tolerant greens like spinach, arugula and mache (corn salad), tatsoi is Doug's No. 1 choice.*

"Tatsoi, a leafy green that is indestructible, is my number one crop for winter," Doug says. "It forms beautiful rosettes of leaves that are so mild that they can be thrown into a salad. Even children will rave about the flavor of the unique spoon-shaped foliage."

Row covers protect edibles from cold temps and harsh wind.

## MAKE THE MOST OF MULCH

An insulating layer of mulch is perhaps the simplest and most cost-effective way to extend the harvest of root crops such as carrots, beets, parsnips and radishes. Before the ground freezes in late autumn, top vegetable beds with a 1-foot thick layer of straw. Cover the mulch with a row cover to prevent it from blowing away. To harvest, lift the fabric, brush aside the mulch, and pull out as many roots as you need.

## FRAME IT UP

Cold frames offer up the most protection and allow for both cool- and cold-season crops to be harvested from early fall through late winter months. This method is simply a bottomless box, typically made from wood and topped with a clear top, such as an old window or a piece of polycarbonate. For maximum sunlight, be sure to slope the clear top toward the south.

### GROW THE RIGHT STUFF

For late harvests, stick to hardy salad greens or root crops, such as carrots or beets, which are seeded in mid- to late summer.

# CHAPTER 8

# Butterflies, Bugs & More

If you've wished you could capture that butterfly in the perfect photo, check out the success stories highlighted here. You'll also learn how to quickly spot the difference between moths and butterflies, where bugs hide out and how to create and cultivate your own beehive.

GLENN TRAVER

# Mighty Small

*Nine butterflies about the size of a thumbprint will make you say "aww."*

**BY HEATHER LAMB**

gardens are full of small delights: spiderwebs shining with morning dew, bird nests tucked into tree limbs, and seedlings nudging up through the soil. But there's something magical about a teeny-tiny butterfly floating through your backyard. Most of the nine species on the next few pages have wingspans of about 1 inch, which means they're no bigger than your thumbprint. By comparison, species such as monarchs and eastern tiger swallowtails are as large as 5 inches across. Experience the thrill of spotting one of these dainty butterflies with this photo roundup.

**WEIGHTING GAME** Just how much does a butterfly weigh? Butterfly field guide author Paul Opler of Colorado State University estimates a large swallowtail weighs 0.3 gram, and smaller butterflies weigh 0.04 gram. The smallest, a pygmy-blue, would weigh only thousandths of a gram. For comparison, a single sugar cube weighs about 3 grams.

Eastern tailed-blue

Gray hairstreak

RICHARD DAY/DAYBREAK IMAGERY (BOTH)

## 1. GRAY HAIRSTREAK

*⅞ to 1⅜ inches*

Host plants include: clover (*Trifolium*), cotton (*Gossypium*) and mallow (*Malvaceae*)

The gray hairstreak is the most common member of this family, ranging across the United States and southern Canada. These rapid fliers are slate gray above and soft gray underneath, with an orange spot near each hindwing tail. They also have white, black and orange streaks.

## 2. EASTERN TAILED-BLUE

*⅞ to 1⅛ inches*

Host plants include: wild pea (*Lathyrus*), yellow sweet clover (*Melilotus officinalis*) and alfalfa (*Medicago sativa*)

Tailed-blues stand out, with beautiful black-edged azure wings and recognizable wing "tails." These fliers flutter low to the ground and feed on smaller flowers because their proboscises are short.

## 3. COMMON CHECKERED-SKIPPER

*1 to 1½ inches*
Host plants include: hollyhock (*Alcea*) and poppy mallow (*Callirhoe*)

Skippers are the sparrows of the butterfly world: There are a lot of them and it's difficult to tell each species apart. The most widespread, the common checkered-skipper, frequents a variety of habitats across much of the U.S. Like other skippers, it has a stout body and is a strong and fast flier.

American copper

## 5. AMERICAN COPPER

*⅞ to 1⅜ inches*
Host plants include: sheep sorrel (*Rumex acetosella*), curled dock (*Rumex crispus*) and mountain sorrel (*Oxyria digyna*)

Although they're not frequent backyard visitors, American coppers are widely distributed across the northern U.S. and southern Canada, often along roadsides or in old fields. The butterflies are a tawny gray above with tigerlike black-spotted orange swathes, and have silvery gray underwings flecked with black.

Harvester

## 4. HARVESTER

*1⅛ to 1¼ inches*
Host plant: none

This resident of eastern stream borders and swamps is no typical garden butterfly. Orange and black on top with tawny spots on the underwings, harvesters often puddle on wet sand. Instead of nectar, adults sip aphid excretions, called honeydew. And harvester caterpillars are carnivorous—they eat aphids instead of plants.

## 6. PEARL CRESCENT

*1¼ to 1¾ inches*
Host plants: several species of asters, such as *Symphyotrichum pilosum var. pilosum* and *Symphyotrichum drummondii var. texanum*

The pearl crescent is part of the brushfoot family, which includes fritillaries, satyrs and the monarch. Smaller than its cousins, this orange and black-checked butterfly is abundant from the East Coast to the Rocky Mountains. The males patrol open areas looking for females and sometimes dart out at intruders.

## 7. DESERT ORANGETIP

*1 to 1½ inches*

Host plants include: tansy-mustard (*Descurainia pinnata*) and tumble mustard (*Sisymbrium altissimum*)

Named for the orange patches on its forewings, the desert orangetip is common in the rocky southwestern desert and might visit gardens with plants from the mustard family, its caterpillar host plant. If the weather is too dry for the orangetip to emerge, it may remain in its chrysalis stage for several years.

## 8. LITTLE METALMARK

*½ to 1 inch*

Host plant: yellow thistle (*Cirsium horridulum*)

The smallest butterfly in this list, the little metalmark has rusty orange wings that are brighter orange underneath. Metallic streaks mark the wings on both sides. It's found in grassy areas along the Gulf Coast and the southeastern Atlantic region. The unique markings make it worth seeking out.

Little metalmark

## 9. DAINTY SULPHUR

*¾ to 1¼ inches*

Host plants include: sneezeweed (*Helenium*), shepherd's needle (*Bidens pilosa*) and cultivated marigold (*Tagetes*)

A list of tiny butterflies wouldn't be complete without the dainty sulphur, the most diminutive of the North American sulphurs. Even its name means "small." Found in open areas across most of the southern U.S., it has distinctive sulphur yellow underwings with three black dots.

# follow the butterflies!

With colorful, intricately patterned wings and long narrow bodies, butterflies make ideal subjects for nature photography. But these fast-flying pollinators dart away in the blink of an eye, which means following them with a camera is quite a challenge. It takes a lot of patience and a little luck to capture a winning shot, like these readers did. Here, they share stories of success.

**An American copper** butterfly stopped at the Lucifer crocosmia in my backyard. Hummingbirds and butterflies love this flower! Nothing beats photographing these tiny fliers on a warm summer day.
**Glenn Traver**
HANOVER TOWNSHIP, PENNSYLVANIA

**Buckeye butterflies typically spend** a lot of time on the ground, but from a distance I saw this one land in my neighbor's garden and grabbed my camera and took several shots before it flew off.
**Edward Leicester**
HERTFORD, NORTH CAROLINA

**This eastern** tiger swallowtail butterfly checked out the coneflower blooms at my family's farm last July. Butterflies usually are a little tattered-looking. I was attracted to this one because it was so perfect. The swallowtail didn't mind as I followed it from flower to flower.
**Tammy Travis**
HANCOCK, WISCONSIN

**One hot afternoon** in June, I went for a hike at Wildcat Ridge Wildlife Management Area in Morris County, New Jersey. Birds were scarce there, but butterflies were everywhere. This great spangled fritillary was one of six butterflies sipping on the sweet blooms, enjoying the bright sun.
**Shayna Marchese**
JERSEY CITY, NEW JERSEY

**When a butterfly** chooses your garden, it's magical. Your cares fade away with each flap of their wings. I grow several flowering plants to attract these beauties. In particular, this zebra longwing needs its host plant, passionflower, for its caterpillars to munch on. As adults, the species enjoys the bright red blossoms of jatropha shrubs and this yellow starry rosinweed.
**Doreen Damm**
NEW PORT RICHEY, FLORIDA

**I love butterflies,** so I attract them with container-grown flowers. I planted milkweed because it's the monarch butterfly's host plant. But one day as I fussed with my flowers, I noticed this white peacock butterfly beautifully perched on the milkweed. I grabbed my camera just in time.
**Donna Chesney**
NAPLES, FLORIDA

**Several monarch** butterflies fed on these blazing star blooms at the same time. It was nature's beauty at its finest.
**Mary Carlson**
PRINCETON, MINNESOTA

## ATTRACT MORE BUTTERFLIES
*Create your own photo ops with these 10 late-blooming plants butterflies can't resist.*

Aster

Autumn Joy sedum

Bee balm

Black-eyed Susan

Chrysanthemum

Goldenrod

Joe Pye weed

Purple coneflower

Russian sage

Zinnia

**A female eastern tiger** swallowtail sipped nectar from a Royal Purple zinnia at the botanical garden at the Riverbanks Zoo in Columbia, South Carolina. I love this photo because of the colors and the butterfly's classic pose.
**Brian Fox**
BLYTHEWOOD, SOUTH CAROLINA

The clubbed antennae of a giant swallowtail tell you it's a butterfly, not a moth.

Hummingbird moths (right) can be mistaken for baby hummingbirds or bumblebees.

# Moth or Butterfly?

*Use these clues to confidently ID the winged creatures you find in your backyard. Here's a hint: Look at the antennae!* **BY SALLY ROTH**

Many people think that moths are the nighttime equivalent of butterflies, but it's not quite that simple. Learn the basic differences between the two fliers so that you can positively say "moth!" or "butterfly!" when you spot one. Keep in mind, though, that most of these characteristics aren't absolute—there are many exceptions to the rules.

One thing you can count on: Butterflies fly only during the day. But not all moths are strictly nighttime fliers. Hummingbird moths, which include several species of sphinx moths, eat nectar at flowers during the day. Others, including colorful buck moths and the *Schinia* species, are also seen when the sun shines.

The best, easiest way to differentiate butterflies from moths is to look at the antennae. All butterflies have long, thin antennae that end in a thickened tip. But no North American moths sport these "clubbed" antennae. Instead, they have shorter,

Giant silk moths have no mouthparts. Their brief life span is for one purpose only: Find a mate and lay eggs. Some moths consume nectar, but this isn't one of them.

feathery antennae—especially prominent on males—that are beautifully plumed and designed to catch wafting pheromones released by females. Female moths typically have simple, thin antennae, similar to a butterfly's at first glance but with a tapered tip.

Notice the difference in posture, too. Butterflies usually hold their wings folded up over their bodies when they rest. They may open and close their wings when feeding on nectar or hold them flat out when basking in sunshine, but folded wings are most common. Nearly all moths rest with their wings flat or folded in a rooflike position over their bodies. Also, their bodies tend to be chubbier than those of butterflies.

Even before these fliers make the transformation into winged adults, several clues can help you determine whether that crawling creature will become a butterfly or

a moth. A fuzzy or hairy caterpillar ambling through your garden is a moth-to-be. Butterfly caterpillars aren't fuzzy or hairy, but they may have spikes. However, if the caterpillar has smooth skin, it could be either.

All butterfly caterpillars transform into a chrysalis, a stage when they have a hard, smooth covering that hangs from a patch of silk on a plant, twig or other

support. On the other hand, moths have cocoons plastered with silk. If you're digging in your garden and uncover a smooth brown cocoon, or pupa, in the soil, it's going to be a moth. No butterfly spends that stage in the soil.

Telling the difference between moths and butterflies is a tricky yet delightful challenge. So head outside and test your newfound knowledge!

## CHEAT SHEET
Decide whether you're looking at a moth or a butterfly.

| MOTH | CHARACTERISTIC | BUTTERFLY |
|---|---|---|
| Feathery | Antennae | Clubbed |
| Often chubby | Body size | Often slim |
| Wings spread flat | Resting posture | Folded wings |
| Night or day | Flight time | Day |
| Fuzzy, hairy or smooth | Caterpillar | Smooth or spiky |

# The
# Mystery

A white-lined sphinx moth sticks out its proboscis, ready to feed on foxglove.

*of*
# SPHINX MOTHS

*These hummingbird look-alikes are fueled by nectar-rich plants that bloom day and night.* **BY SALLY ROTH**

W atch sphinx moths flitting around your flowers and you'll know why they're often called hummingbird moths. Some species look so much like the tiny birds, right down to the green body and whirring wings, that it's easy to mistake one for a hovering hummer. You also may know sphinx moths as hawk moths, because their streamlined wings make them fast and agile fliers.

While some sphinx species take the day shift, others work after the sun goes down. Clear-winged types, which mimic hummingbirds, bees or wasps, fly only during the day. They hover to feed at plants such as butterfly bush (*Buddleia davidii*), honeysuckle vines (*Lonicera sempervirens*) or other flowers that are nectar-rich.

Dusk through dark is prime time for most sphinx species. That's when to look for five-spotted hawk moths hovering at petunias, hostas, four-o'clocks, and other tubular flowers. Night fliers, including the banded sphinx, start their shift at dark.

Moths such as the white-lined sphinx and nessus sphinx are busiest when the sun sinks but pull double duty and also seek nectar during the day.

To maximize the sphinx moth population in your backyard, simply grow a variety of plants that bloom in both day and night hours. Like hummingbirds, sphinx moths prefer tube-shaped flowers with nectar in the base of the petals, such as columbines, nasturtiums and four-o'clocks. That structure prevents many other pollinators from draining the nectar dry, so the chance of a payoff is much greater than in daisies or other flowers that butterflies or

**THE CLEARWING**
sphinx moth often stumps gardeners. At first glance, many think it is a hummingbird or a bumblebee.

A hummingbird clearwing at a butterfly bush

This snowberry clearwing moth in its caterpillar stage found a safe place on a honeysuckle.

**TICKLE A SPHINX** moth caterpillar and the larva will rear up defensively, curling its head while the rest of its body remains flat. This is the same posture taken by the mythical beasts that guard pharaohs' tombs.

Big poplar
sphinx moth

**THE BIG POPLAR** sphinx, with wings 4 to nearly 6 inches across, has no proboscis at all! It never feeds in its adult stage but emerges only to locate a mate and start the next generation.

bees easily visit. Plus, sphinx moths have a secret weapon: an extra-long proboscis, or drinking straw, that is sometimes twice the length of their body. The proboscis allows them to reach nectar in plants that other pollinators can't.

Unlike hummingbirds, however, sphinx moths don't zero in on red. Tubular flowers in any color lure day-fliers, while fragrant white or light-colored blossoms hail the sphinx moth squad in the evening by both sight and scent. Flowers such as four-o'clocks and moonflower that open late in the day or at night, or ones that release a stronger fragrance at night, such as honeysuckle and petunias, attract the evening shift. Plant a trellis of moonflower vine (*Ipomoea alba*) or place a potted datura on your patio to watch the blossoms unfurl at dusk. If you're lucky, the moths will arrive minutes later.

Choosing moth-friendly blooms is worth the effort it takes when the reward is a glance at one of these peculiar fliers. The wings of clear-winged sphinx moths, such as the snowberry clearwing, become

clear soon after emerging from the cocoon. Other species conceal their beauty under a pair of brown or gray patterned top wings for protective coloration. When open wide, their underwings are beautiful—often a rosy pink, sometimes with deep blue eyespots as sported by the twin-spotted sphinx.

No matter how gorgeous the adults, the larvae evoke a "Yuck!" from many, although not from birds, which eagerly devour them. When full-grown, the caterpillars are about the size of your little finger and are smooth with a pointy horn at the tail end.

It's normal to overlook the unseemly larvae entirely unless one crosses your path as it walks off to pupate in late summer or early fall. Or you may only notice its presence when you see your tomato leaves have been devoured by a hungry caterpillar.

But it's a real treat when an adult sphinx chooses to feed on backyard plants. Whether you watch one at your flowers during the day or catch a glimpse of one darting through the night, the secrets of the sphinx moths are a thrill to uncover.

Five-spotted hawk
moth caterpillar, also
known as a tomato
hornworm

# 18 Plants to Attract Sphinx Moths

### NECTAR PLANTS

Brugmansia

Butterfly bush

Columbine

Datura

Evening primrose

Flowering tobacco (*Nicotiana*)

Four-o'clocks

Honeysuckle

Hosta

Moonflower vine (*Ipomoea alba*)

Nasturtium

Verbena

### HOST PLANTS

Grapevine

Honeysuckle

Poplar (*Populus* species, including cottonwood, poplar, aspen)

Snowberry (*Symphoricarpos species*)

Virginia creeper

Tomato

Five-spotted hawk moth

# Tucked Away for Winter

*Butterflies and bugs make themselves at home nestled under leaves or hidden beneath tree bark in the backyard.* **BY KENN AND KIMBERLY KAUFMAN**

As snow melts, adult mourning cloak butterflies emerge from winter hibernation.

Monarchs perform one of the most famous migrations in the world, but not all of their fellow fliers escape to the south. Most butterflies and most other insects don't migrate. They're hidden in the landscape in various stages of their life cycles for the winter months. Here's how and where some of your favorite backyard guests withstand the chilly weather.

## SURVIVAL SKILLS

Butterflies and other bugs use various mechanisms to make it through the brutally cold months. They slow their metabolisms way down in a process called diapause. Certain chemicals in their bodies act as antifreeze. And they rid their bodies of nearly all water to avoid turning into an ice crystal.

## LIFE STAGES

Some butterflies hibernate through winter as adults. Mourning cloaks, question marks, commas and others hunker down, tucked away behind loose bark or in fallen leaves. But most spend the season in other stages of their life cycle.

Fritillaries, crescents and many skippers hatch in the fall and sleep through winter as caterpillars. Other species, such as coral hairstreaks and Karner blues, overwinter as eggs and hatch the following spring. Viceroys, also known as monarch look-alikes, employ an entirely different tactic. Caterpillars from the summer's last brood create shelters called hibernacula. The itty-bitty caterpillars instinctively know to chew a leaf in a specific pattern, then fold and fashion it into a tentlike structure. The rolled leaf is lined and fastened to a stalk with silk the caterpillars spin themselves. Other caterpillars, like the beautiful and well-known swallowtails, reach full size and form their pupa, or chrysalis, before winter sets in.

Common backyard bugs persevere in similar ways. Many moth and beetle eggs, for example, are hidden in rough tree bark or under leaf litter. Praying mantis eggs stay safe and cozy in insulated egg sacs. Most dragonflies in their wingless nymph stage survive the cold underwater. And if your house has ever been invaded by swarms of lady beetles or stinkbugs in fall, then you know their overwintering strategy all too well.

## WINTER HIDEOUTS

The more habitat you supply for butterflies and other insects, the more robust with the flying creatures your spring garden will be. It's as simple as not being too tidy. Dried plant stalks and seed heads offer hiding spots for insects, so go easy on deadheading. Stacks of firewood, brush piles and leaf litter also make a backyard more desirable to bugs.

Before you know it, higher temps wake backyard insects, and your space comes alive again.

# How Butterflies Work

*Zoom in and discover how these pretty little fliers gracefully flutter through your garden.*  **BY KAITLIN STAINBROOK**

*Proboscis: a long, hollow tube for drinking nectar (shown coiled)*

*Clubbed antenna: provides orientation and sense of smell*

*Legs: six total, sometimes of different sizes*

*Head*

*Compound eye: detects color and movement*

*Forewing*

*Thorax: where the wings and legs attach*

*Abdomen*

*Hindwing*

**THE WONDER OF WINGS**
If you put a butterfly wing under a microscope, you'll see that it is actually covered in many tiny scales, which give the butterfly its colors and patterns. Underneath the scales are thin layers of protein called chitin, which is also found in octopus beaks, insect exoskeletons, fish scales and more.

# Adventures in Beekeeping

*It's easy to go from zero to bee hero.*
*Follow this newbie's journey to learn how*
*to get your backyard abuzz.*
BY MELINDA MYERS

Queen bee
with a tag

## THE PAINFUL TRUTH

It's true that if you become a beekeeper, you will occasionally get stung. But a honeybee sting is not nearly as painful as being stung by a wasp, and there are a lot of precautions you can take, like using a smoker and donning protective clothing. It's also helpful to move slowly around the hive, avoid swatting at the bees, and open the hive only on warm days when most of the bees are out foraging. Beekeepers will tell you that the fresh honey and productive gardens are more than worth the occasional sting.

## "I've always wanted to raise bees."

That offhand comment was all it took for my friend Pete to give me a beekeeping gift, complete with bee box and how-to books, for Mother's Day two years ago. But Pete's thoughtful present arrived a little late to order bees, so it sat on a shelf in the garage for a year.

Last spring, my daughter told a beekeeper about my failure to launch, and the next thing I knew, two enthusiastic beekeepers, Cesar Cerna and Carol Kremer, were buzzing around my yard, ready to get my hive off the ground. Beekeepers for seven years, they learned by attending beekeeping workshops. Now they pay it forward and mentor newbies like me.

The first thing I needed was a complete bee box. I had only a 10-frame super (the structure to hold the bees), but I lacked other critical items such as inner and outer covers, a bottom and a stand. I also didn't have a protective veil or gloves. Or bees. But Cesar and Carol patiently helped me order everything I needed. Cesar also lent me a top for the box, and Carol lent her sugar-water jar, which is used to feed the bees

until they get comfy in their new home and start foraging on their own.

One thing I did have was the perfect sunny spot for the hive among the fruit trees and flowers in my large garden. Sheltered inside a fenced area, it's also safe from strong winds and hungry animals.

I started my hive with a nucleus colony, which is fully established with a fertilized queen, larvae, combs and honey. The queen is larger than the others; her wings cover only two-thirds of her body. We located her nestled among the drones, which mate with the queen, and the worker bees, which guard the hive and collect nectar.

We set the five-frame nucleus colony inside the 10-frame super, added the lid, set out the sugar water and let the bees settle into their new home. After a week or two, Cesar and Carol came back to check on the queen. We needed to make sure she hadn't packed her bags instead of producing offspring. It didn't take much searching to find white ricelike eggs and healthy, pearly white larvae and pupae in capped cells. Things were

1. Smoking the hive calms the bees.
2. The bees don't mind as the top of the hive is removed.
3. Delicious honey is close at hand when the first frame is lifted up.
4. A beekeeper opens the wax-capped honeycombs with a hot knife and lets the honey flow.

## A BEEKEEPER'S TOOL KIT

*Get the right supplies for success!*

○ **Bee brush:** helps gently move bees out of the way during hive inspections
○ **Hive tool:** a mini pry bar for lifting off the sealed top and frames for inspections
○ **Jacket with veil and gloves:** protective clothing that increases your comfort level when working with bees
○ **Smoker:** calms bees, reducing the beekeeper's risk of being stung
○ **Super:** a box with eight to 10 frames where bees build honeycombs

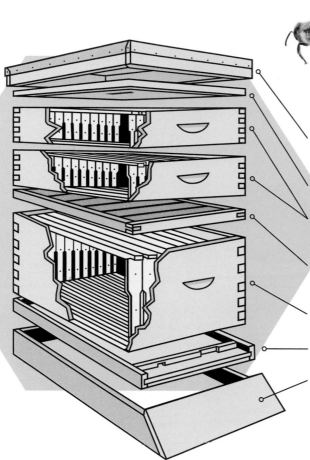

## HOME SWEET HOME
*Take a tour of a honeybee's hive.*

**OUTER COVER** sits on top of the hive to protect bees from harsh weather

**INNER COVER** goes over the uppermost super

**HONEY SUPERS** contain frames for honey storage

**QUEEN EXCLUDER** prevents the queen from laying eggs in honey supers

**DEEP SUPER** contains frames to house bees

**BOTTOM BOARD** is the floor of the hive

**STAND** elevates the hive to reduce any damage to the bottom board from dampness

going so well, I had to expand their home with another super to give the bees more space.

I was excited to find many of the bees visiting my flowerbeds. On hot days, I saw clusters near the hive entrance. Cesar assured me this was normal behavior during hot weather. He said it was called bearding, which is when some worker bees exit the hive to keep things cooler inside. They fan their wings to move cooler air into and through the hive.

About two months in, it was time to add a half-super for the bees to store honey. Although the colony had been coming along nicely, we belatedly realized that the hive was leaning to one side. The wooden stand was not holding up to outdoor conditions as well as we'd hoped. Pete and I put a new one together, this time made of tough cement blocks so it would be sure to last.

It was a perfectly simple solution, but then we ran into a different problem: how to transfer the heavy bee- and honey-filled hive to its new stand. We definitely didn't want to agitate the bees. But Cesar and

Carol came to the rescue once again. We smoked the hive to keep the bees calm during the move. The smoke hinders their sense of smell, which bees use to communicate. Normally, if there's a hive intruder, bees release an alarm pheromone to ready a group attack. If they can't smell the pheromone, they stay calm.

Cesar was excited to share the hive progress with Pete, and he handed him a bee-filled frame once the bees were soothed. Pete had not expected to be quite so involved with my beekeeping adventure!

Then it was time to hold the bee-filled super, which probably weighed over 50 pounds. Pete later told me that he was so focused on the risk of an angry bee flying up his shorts that he didn't even notice how heavy the super was. The good news is that none of us, including the bees, were harmed during the move.

Once everyone was settled in again, the super filled up fast, and I added a second one a month later. I left the honey for the bees this first year so they'd have plenty of food to get them through the winter. Straw bales now surround the hive to keep the bees warm during the cold Wisconsin weather. They'll huddle inside to live off their honey stores until next spring, when the flowers will bloom and my honeybees will return to my backyard garden.

# Light up the Night

*When the sun goes down, fireflies glow. Read on to learn more about these extraordinary insects.* **BY KAITLIN STAINBROOK**

**100,000**

*Actual fireflies are scarce around bustling Tokyo, Japan, but one firefly festival releases 100,000 small glowing orbs on the Sumida River to imitate that quintessential glow.*

**1** From 1960 to the mid-1990s, the Sigma Chemical Co. paid collectors up to one penny per firefly, harvesting over 100 million lightning bugs and possibly reducing local populations. (The company sold luciferase, which is the enzyme that produces light in fireflies.)

**1** *In Great Smoky Mountains National Park in Tennessee, one particular species of firefly* (Photinus carolinus) *synchronizes to create some beautiful bioluminescent displays.*

**21** Lightning bugs live as adults for about 21 days.

**0** If a field is paved over, the fireflies that lived there don't migrate to another field. Instead, they disappear entirely.

**100** Nearly 100 percent of the chemical reaction in a firefly's abdomen is released as light. They glow to find a mate, communicate with members of their species, and to show predators that they are distasteful.

**3** Firefly light comes in three different colors: yellow, orange and green.

This flowering quince is home to a small paper wasp nest.

Paper wasps fiercely protect the inhabitants of their nests.

# The Wonder of Wasps

*Meet one of your best allies in pest control.*

BY SALLY ROTH

It's easy to think of wasps as the annoying yellow jackets that raid your backyard barbecue, or the paper wasps that build nests under your eaves. But in reality, social wasps are your best allies in pest control, and they rarely sting people.

In fact, only 38 wasp species sting aggressively, and that's because they have helpless eggs, larvae and pupae to defend in their nests. The rest of North America's 14,500 wasp species are shy, solitary types like mud daubers, sand wasps and cicada killers.

What surprises most people about wasps is that, just like bees and butterflies, they're pollinators, too. For example, pollen wasps actively gather pollen from penstemon west of the Rocky Mountains. And although plenty of wasps visit flowers merely seeking nectar to fuel their flight, they still end up spreading pollen from bloom to bloom as a result.

Another benefit of wasps is that they eat pesky bugs that might otherwise infest your garden. Instead of weevils,

## WELCOME WASPS
*Follow our tips to attract these industrious bugs to your yard.*

- Avoid using pesticides in your backyard or garden.

- Landscape with native trees, shrubs and flowers.

- Install a bee condo. A simple wood block drilled with holes of various diameters offers housing to solitary wasps.

- Accept aphids. They secrete a liquid called honeydew that wasps crave, especially in fall when there are fewer flowers with nectar.

A solitary wasp visits a flower in the arid climate of the Southwest.

aphids, cutworms, grasshoppers and stinkbugs munching on your backyard veggies, these pests end up being on the menu themselves.

The potential for wasp stings makes many people nervous, but male wasps actually lack stingers. For the female wasps that sting, you can take simple precautions to avoid the pain. Inspect birdhouses, overturned flowerpots and other concealed locations in your yard where a wasp might make its nest. And before you rev up your lawnmower, investigate for hidden nests in trees, rock walls and rodent burrows. If you find a nest you don't want, contact a professional bee-removal service to destroy it for you.

Not only are wasps very capable pollinators and pest-destroyers, they're master architects, too. The paper combs made by social wasps are composed of hexagonal cells, which conserve labor and materials while maximizing space. Yellow jackets enclose their combs in a multi-layered paper envelope that insulates against extreme weather. And solitary potter wasps craft marble-sized urns of mud. It's hard not to be at least a little bit in awe of their industry.

The next time you see a wasp in your backyard, be thankful. They truly are vital to a healthy landscape and, once you take the time to watch them in action, are endlessly fascinating.

## THE SOCIAL SCENE
The difference between social and solitary wasps is that social wasps tend to be predators that build large nests and are willing to aggressively defend them. There is one reproductive individual supported by hundreds of female "workers." Solitary wasps either lay eggs in a host nest or build small nests they don't typically try to protect.

*Zebra swallowtail*
Finalist in our Backyard Photo Contest
**PHOTO BY LAURA FRAZIER**

Giant swallowtail
Finalist in our Backyard Photo Contest
**PHOTO BY TAMMI FRICK**

Monarch
**PHOTO BY DESIGN PICS INC/ALAMY STOCK PHOTO**

Monarch caterpillar
**PHOTO BY RICHARD DAY/DAYBREAK IMAGERY**

# Native Plants Chart

*Attract more birds and butterflies by including native plants in your landscape.*

| | COMMON NAME | SCIENTIFIC NAME | HARDINESS ZONES | FLOWER COLOR | HEIGHT | BLOOM TIME | SOIL MOISTURE |
|---|---|---|---|---|---|---|---|
| **DRY SOILS AND DRY CLIMATES (15"–25" ANNUAL PRECIPITATION)** | **Leadplant** | *Amorpha canescens* | 3-8 | Purple | 2' - 3' | June-July | D, M |
| | **Butterfly weed** | *Asclepias tuberosa* | 3-10 | Orange | 2' - 3' | June-Aug. | D, M |
| | **Smooth aster** | *Aster laevis* | 4-8 | Blue | 2' - 4' | Aug.-Oct. | D, M |
| | **Cream false indigo** | *Baptisia bracteata* | 4-9 | Cream | 1' - 2' | May-June | D, M |
| | **Purple prairie clover** | *Dalea purpurea* | 3-8 | Purple | 1' - 2' | July-Aug. | D, M |
| | **Pale purple coneflower** | *Echinacea pallida* | 4-8 | Purple | 3' - 5' | June-July | D, M |
| | **Prairie smoke** | *Geum triflorum* | 3-6 | Pink | 6" | May-June | D, M |
| | **Dotted blazing star** | *Liatris punctata* | 3-9 | Purple/Pink | 1' - 2' | Aug.-Oct. | D, M |
| | **Wild lupine** | *Lupinus perennis* | 3-8 | Blue | 1' - 2' | May-June | D |
| | **Large-flowered beardtongue** | *Penstemon grandiflorus* | 3-7 | Lavender | 2' - 4' | May-June | D |
| | **Showy goldenrod** | *Solidago speciosa* | 3-8 | Yellow | 1' - 3' | Aug.-Sept. | D, M |
| | **Bird's-foot violet** | *Viola pedata* | 3-9 | Blue | 6" | Apr.-June | D |
| **MEDIUM SOILS IN AVERAGE RAINFALL CLIMATES (25"–45" ANNUAL PRECIPITATION)** | **Nodding pink onion** | *Allium cernuum* | 3-8 | White/Pink | 1' - 2' | July-Aug. | M, Mo |
| | **New England aster** | *Aster novae-angliae* | 3-7 | Blue/Purple | 3' - 6' | Aug.-Sept. | M, Mo |
| | **Blue false indigo** | *Baptisia australis* | 3-10 | Blue | 3' - 5' | June-July | M, Mo |
| | **White false indigo** | *Baptisia lactea* | 4-9 | White | 3' - 5' | June-July | M, Mo |
| | **Shooting star** | *Dodecatheon meadia* | 4-8 | White/Pink | 1' - 2' | May-June | M, Mo |
| | **Purple coneflower** | *Echinacea purpurea* | 4-8 | Purple | 3' - 4' | July-Sept. | M, Mo |
| | **Rattlesnake master** | *Eryngium yuccifolium* | 4-9 | White | 3' - 5' | June-Aug. | M |
| | **Prairie blazing star** | *Liatris pycnostachya* | 3-9 | Purple/Pink | 3' - 5' | July-Aug. | M, Mo |
| | **Wild quinine** | *Parthenium integrifolium* | 4-8 | White | 3' - 5' | June-Sept. | M, Mo |
| | **Yellow coneflower** | *Ratibida pinnata* | 3-9 | Yellow | 3' - 6' | July-Sept. | M, Mo |
| | **Royal catchfly** | *Silene regia* | 4-9 | Red | 2' - 4' | July-Aug. | M |
| | **Stiff goldenrod** | *Solidago rigida* | 3-9 | Yellow | 3' - 5' | Aug.-Sept. | M, Mo |
| **MOIST SOILS AND MOIST CLIMATES (45"–60" ANNUAL PRECIPITATION)** | **Wild hyacinth** | *Camassia scilloides* | 4-8 | White | 1' - 2' | May-June | M, Mo |
| | **Tall Joe Pye weed** | *Eupatorium fistulosum* | 4-9 | Purple/Pink | 5' - 8' | Aug.-Sept. | Mo, W |
| | **Queen of the prairie** | *Filipendula rubra* | 3-6 | Pink | 4' - 5' | June-July | M, Mo |
| | **Bottle gentian** | *Gentiana andrewsii* | 3-6 | Blue | 1' - 2' | Aug.-Oct. | Mo, W |
| | **Rose mallow** | *Hibiscus palustris* | 4-9 | Pink | 3' - 6' | July-Sept. | Mo, W |
| | **Dense blazing star** | *Liatris spicata* | 4-10 | Purple/Pink | 3' - 6' | Aug.-Sept. | Mo, W |
| | **Cardinal flower** | *Lobelia cardinalis* | 3-9 | Red | 2' - 5' | July-Sept. | Mo, W |
| | **Marsh phlox** | *Phlox glaberrima* | 4-8 | Red/ Purple | 2' - 4' | June-July | M, Mo |
| | **Sweet black-eyed Susan** | *Rudbeckia subtomentosa* | 3-9 | Yellow | 4' - 6' | Aug.-Oct. | M, Mo |
| | **Ohio goldenrod** | *Solidago ohioensis* | 4-5 | Yellow | 3' - 4' | Aug.-Sept. | M, Mo |
| | **Tall ironweed** | *Vernonia altissima* | 4-9 | Red/Pink | 5' - 8' | Aug.-Sept. | Mo, W |
| | **Culver's root** | *Veronicastrum virginicum* | 3-8 | White | 3' - 6' | July-Aug. | M, Mo |

**SOIL MOISTURE KEY**

**D** = Dry (Well-draining sandy and rocky soils), **M** = Medium (Normal garden soils such as loam, sandy loam and clay loam),

**Mo** = Moist (Soils that stay moist below the surface, but are not boggy; may dry out in late summer),

**W** = Wet (Soils that are continually moist through the growing season, subject to short periods of spring flooding)

# What's Your Zone?

## *Plant Hardiness Zone Map*

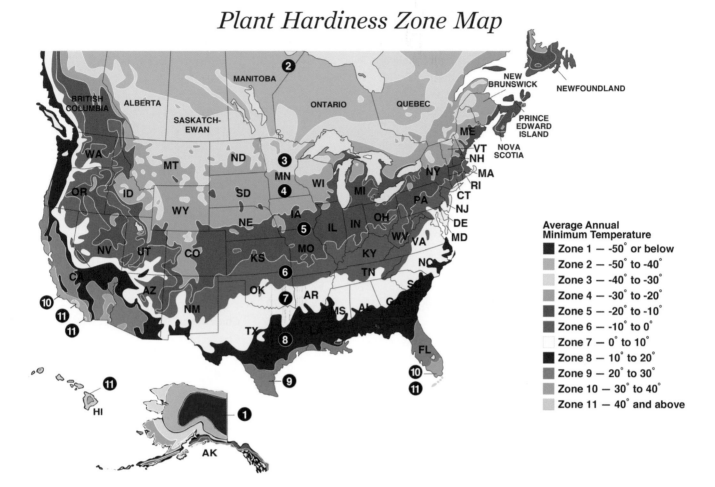

**Average Annual Minimum Temperature**

- Zone 1 — -50° or below
- Zone 2 — -50° to -40°
- Zone 3 — -40° to -30°
- Zone 4 — -30° to -20°
- Zone 5 — -20° to -10°
- Zone 6 — -10° to 0°
- Zone 7 — 0° to 10°
- Zone 8 — 10° to 20°
- Zone 9 — 20° to 30°
- Zone 10 — 30° to 40°
- Zone 11 — 40° and above

## *Plant Heat Zone Map*

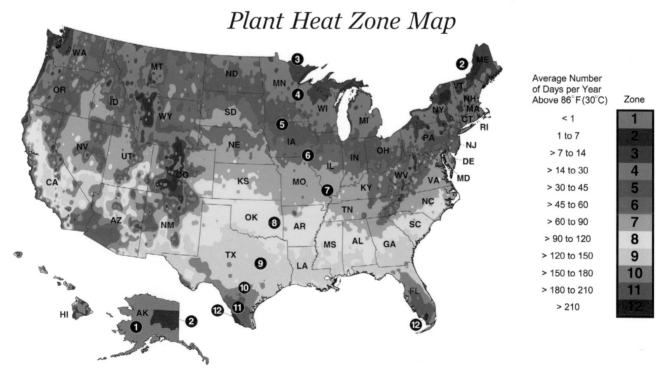

**Average Number of Days per Year Above 86° F (30°C)** — **Zone**

- < 1 — 1
- 1 to 7 — 2
- > 7 to 14 — 3
- > 14 to 30 — 4
- > 30 to 45 — 5
- > 45 to 60 — 6
- > 60 to 90 — 7
- > 90 to 120 — 8
- > 120 to 150 — 9
- > 150 to 180 — 10
- > 180 to 210 — 11
- > 210 — 12

Maps courtesy of the USDA and American Horticultural Society. The zones featured should be treated as general guidelines when selecting plants for your garden. For more information on your specific region visit: usna.usda.gov/Hardzone

# Index

> " *The reason birds can fly and we can't is simply because they have perfect faith, for to have faith is to have wings.* "
> —J.M. BARRIE

Tufted
titmouse